BEHIND THE
HEADLINES

BEHIND THE HEADLINES

Great Moments in
American Newspaper History

Thomas Fleming

DOUBLEDAY & COMPANY, INC.
1970

CONTENTS

1. First Fights for Freedom   1

2. Freedom Goes Too Far   13

3. First of the Giants   28

4. The Reporter's War   38

5. New Giants and New Frontiers   54

6. Last of the Little Wars   68

7. To the Western Front   78

8. Making Readers Care   92

9. Courage on Land and Sea   106

10. On the Job Around the World   119

Index   132

1. FIRST FIGHTS FOR FREEDOM

Out of the murky April dawn that still shrouded the Lexington town green loomed a column of British troops. A straggling line of some seventy or eighty American militiamen stretched across the damp grass, blocking their line of march. Another forty or fifty spectators stood around the edges of the tree-lined patch of grass. Among them was a man named Isaiah Thomas. Watching, he experienced bitter unbelieving horror and fierce outrage when first one gun and then another barked and the infuriated British blasted more than a dozen Americans to the ground with a ragged volley, then charged them with the bayonet.

Isaiah Thomas was one of hundreds of Americans who shouldered a musket and fought through the heat of that blazing day, avenging the men he had seen crumple to the grass in that momentous dawn. But when the battle was over, he did not go back to his farm to recall the day as a proud memory to tell his children and grandchildren. Tall, husky, handsome, Isaiah Thomas, only twenty-six on April 19, 1775, was a newspaperman. Since 1770 he had been typesetter, reporter and editor of the Massachusetts *Spy*, considered the finest of the thirty-seven newspapers then

being published in the American colonies. Almost from the
first edition Thomas became one of that small band of
tough-minded Bostonians who dared to defy the power of
the British Crown.

Two days before the fighting broke out at Lexington,
he learned that the British were about to close his paper
and arrest him for high treason. With the aid of his burly
friend Paul Revere, he had taken apart his press and
smuggled it and a precious supply of paper out of Boston
the following night. He was one of the few who watched
the tower of Old North Church that same night for the two
flashing lanterns that meant the British were coming by
water.

Now in Watertown, where he had taken his press,
Thomas worked frantically day and night to get it back
into operation. Soon thousands in Massachusetts and other
colonies—in those days papers were passed from hand to
hand and a single copy was read by hundreds—were ex-
citedly discussing the eyewitness account of America's first
war correspondent.

About 10 o'clock on the night of the 18th of April,
the troops in Boston were disclosed to be on the move
in a very secret manner and it was found they were em-
barking on boats (which they privately brought to the place
in the evening) at the bottom of the Common; expresses
set off immediately to alarm the country, that they might
be on their guard. When the expresses got about a mile
beyond Lexington, they were stopped by about 14 officers
on horseback, who came out of Boston in the afternoon
of that day, and were seen lurking in by-places in the
country till after dark. One of the expresses immediately

fled, and was pursued two miles by an officer, who when he had got up with him presented a pistol and told him he was a dead man if he did not stop, but he rode on until he came to a house, whence stopping of a sudden his horse threw him off, having the presence of mind to halloo to the people in the house,

"Turn out. Turn out. I have got one of them."

The officer immediately retreated and fled as fast as he had pursued. The other express, after passing through a strict examination, by some means got clear.

The body of troops in the meantime, under the command of Lieutenant Colonel Smith, had crossed the river and landed at Phipps Farm. They immediately, to the number of 1,000, proceeded to Lexington, about six miles below Concord, with great silence. A company of militia, of about 80 men, mustered near the Meeting House; the troops came in sight of them just before sunrise. The militia, upon seeing the troops, began to disperse. The troops then set out upon the run, hallooing and hussaing, and coming within a few rods of them, the commanding officer accosted the militia, in words to this effect,

"Disperse, you damn rebels—damn you, disperse."

Upon which the troops again hussaed, and immediately one or two officers discharged their pistols, which were simultaneously followed by the firing of four or five of the soldiers; and then there seemed to be a general discharge from the whole body. Eight of our men were killed and nine wounded.

The early part of the story, about the escape of the first express rider, could only have been written by a reporter who got it from the lips of the man himself—Paul Revere's forgotten partner, William Dawes. The second express rider was Revere himself, whom Thomas obviously did not have time to interview. But in these early years newspapermen were not especially interested in reporting the news precisely as it happened. Men were only beginning to discover what a newspaper was, what it could do, what it could become.

By the time the American Revolution exploded on an astonished world, they had learned one thing: a newspaper was a political weapon that could change men's minds. When Patrick Henry thundered a warning to George III before a small group of aristocrats in the Virginia House of Burgesses in 1765, only a comparative handful would have heard about it if the story had not been published in the Virginia *Gazette*. In Boston around the same time, violent opposition to British taxation was led by another *Gazette* printed by Benjamin Edes and John Gill. Famous names in American history, Samuel Adams, his cousin John Adams, James Otis, John Hancock, wrote for it. When the royal governor attempted to indict the two publishers for libel, the Massachusetts House of Representatives passed a notable declaration: "The liberty of the press is a great bulwark of the liberty of the people: It is therefore the incumbent duty of those who are constituted the guardians of the people's rights to defend and maintain it."

When the *Gazette*'s circulation soared to a record-breaking two thousand, the governor lamented, "Seven-eighths of the people read none but this infamous paper." A few years later, His Britannic Majesty's representatives thought even less of Edes and Gill. It was in the newspaper's offices that the members of the Boston Tea Party donned their Indian disguises.

The idea of a newspaper as a "political engine" (as

John Adams called it) was by no means new to Americans. More than once, in the decades before the Revolution, newspapermen had risked their livelihoods and even their lives to combat venal officials and other enemies of the body politic. Among the first were James Franklin and his younger brother Ben, who founded a Boston paper called the *Courant*. They battled for freedom to criticize the leaders of the Congregational Church, which dominated the government of Massachusetts. "There are many persons who seem to be more than ordinarily religious," James declared in the *Courant*, "but yet are on several accounts worse, by far, than those who pretend to no religion at all." For this and other remarks, James was jailed for a time and forbidden not only to publish his paper, but "any other pamphlet or paper of the like nature, except it first be supervised by the Secretary of this Province."

James Franklin's jail sentence gave his more gifted younger brother Ben a chance to try his skills as a newsman. It was a notable moment in American newspaper history, not so much for any particular event he reported, but for the new dimension which he added to newspapers—humor. When news ran short, as it often did, printers in these early days filled up their pages with scraps of philosophic writing and excerpts from windy sermons. Franklin had other ideas. On February 11, 1723, the paper was transferred to his name, to escape the magistrate's ban on his brother James, and the new publisher announced a new policy.

The present undertaking . . . is designed purely for the diversion and merriment of the reader. Pieces of pleasancy

and mirth have a secret charm in them to allay the heats
and humours of our spirits, and to make a man forget his
restless resentments. They have a strange power to tune the
harsh disorders of the soul, and to reduce us to a serene
and placid state of mind. The main design of this weekly
paper will be to entertain the town with the most comical
and diverting incidents of humane life.

Franklin promptly proved that he meant what he said,
by producing a witty essay, making fun of the eighteenth
century's love of titles. In it, one could see the first glimmer-
ings of the older man, who became one of the leaders of the
American Revolution.

In old time it was no disrespect for men and women
to be called by their own names. Adam was never called
Master Adam; we never read of Noah Esquire . . . nor
the Right Honorable Abraham, Viscount Mesopotamia,
Baron of Canaan. No, no, they were plain men, honest
country graziers, that took care of their families and their
flocks. Moses was a great prophet and Aaron a priest of
the Lord; but we never read of the Reverend Moses nor
the Right Reverend Father in God, Aaron, by Divine Provi-
dence Lord Archbishop of Israel. Thou never sawest Madam
Rebecca in the Bible, My Lady Rachel; nor Mary, though
a princess of the blood, after the death of Joseph called
the Princess Dowager of Nazareth. No, plain Rebecca,
Rachel, Mary, or the Widow Mary, or the like.

Not long after, Franklin migrated to Philadelphia, and
a few years later began his own paper, the Pennsylvania
Gazette. Completely his own boss now, he livened his paper
with all sorts of funny stories and advertisements. Among

his favorite tricks was the running story, that kept readers going from week to week. One day he published the following ad:

> Pray let the prettiest creature in this place know by publishing this that if it was not for her affectation she would be absolutely irresistible.

The following week the ladies of Philadelphia replied:

> Mr. Franklin, I cannot conceive who your Correspondent means by the prettiest Creature in this Place; but I can assure either him or her, that she who is truly so, has no Affectation at all.
>
> Sir, Since your last week's Paper I have look'd in my Glass a thousand times, I believe, in one Day; and if it was not for the Charge of Affectation I might, without partiality, believe myself the Person meant.
>
> Mr. Franklin, I must own that several have told me, I am the prettiest Creature in this Place; but I believe I shou'd not have been tax'd with Affectation if I cou'd have thought as well of them as they do of themselves. Sir: your Sex calls me pretty; my own affected. Is it from Judgment in the one, or Envy in the other?
>
> Mr. Franklin, They that call me affected are greatly mistaken; for I don't know that I ever refus'd a kiss to any Body but a Fool.
>
> Friend Benjamin, I am not at all displeased at being charged with Affectation. Thou know'st the vain People call Decency of Behavior by that name.

Even his news stories had the ring, and sometimes the sting of wit in them.

An unhappy man; one Sturgis, upon some Difference with his Wife determined to drown himself in the River, and she (Kind Wife) went with him, it seems to see it faithfully performed, and accordingly stood by silent and unconcerned during the whole transaction: he jumped near Carpenter's Wharf, but was timely taken out again before what he came about was thoroughly effected, so that they were both obliged to return home as they came and put up for that time with the disappointment.

On March 16, 1732, Franklin printed this little story:

A servant girl near Christine Bridge hanged herself lately with a design, as 'tis thought to haunt a young fellow who refused to marry her.

The *Gazette* was always full of letters to the editor, frequently composed by its publisher. Among the more enjoyable was the sad story of Anthony Afterwit, whose shrewish wife spent him into bankruptcy, and Celia Single, another born shrew who lectured the editor in scorching terms because of his partiality to men. Even better was Alice Addertongue, who announced that she was organizing a kind of stock exchange for the sale and transfer of calumnies, slanders and other reputation-wrecking pastimes of the gentler sex.

Then there was the worried reader who asked the editor the following question: "If A found out that his neighbor B was sleeping with his wife, was he justified in telling B's wife and persuading her to seek a little revenge with A?"

The editor's reply: "If an ass kicks me, should I kick him again?"

Franklin carried on a long, lively war with his chief competitor, the *Mercury*, winning round after round by making his readers laugh at his rival. He printed a letter from a man who declared himself the author of some verses published in the last edition of the *Mercury*. The fellow complained that for some incomprehensible reason the editor of the *Mercury*, Andrew Bradford, had printed only the first two letters of his name, B.L. "I request you to inform the Publick that I did not desire my name should be conceal'd," the purported author wrote, "and that the remaining letters are O, C, K, H, E, A, D." Another letter pointed out that the *Mercury* had reported two prominent European soldiers had been killed by a single cannon ball —a remarkable achievement, when one of them was fighting in the Rhineland and the other in Italy.

Franklin also cherished a rugged spirit of independence. Only early in his newspaper career, when he was dueling with Andrew Bradford's *Mercury*, several of his friends came in a delegation to warn him to moderate his views. Bradford was siding with the so-called Proprietary party, those who supported the rule of William Penn's sons, who ran Pennsylvania as their semipublic inheritance. Franklin sided with the people against the self-interested politics of the Proprietors. As soon as Franklin saw what the delegation had in mind, he said he was too busy to listen to them at the moment, but would be happy to hear their dire predictions if they would join him for dinner at his house. That night the doomsters showed up at Franklin's table. They

were baffled when his wife, Deborah, served them nothing
but a bowl of strange-looking mush, and a pitcher of cold
water. Franklin spooned the mush into his dish, poured
himself a glass of water and began to eat. The warners
tried to follow his example, but again and again they found
themselves gagging in the midst of their cautionary
speeches. Franklin, meanwhile, spooned down the mush
without so much as a grimace. Finally, they could stand it
no longer and asked him what in the world they were
eating.

"Sawdust meal and water," Franklin snapped. "Now go
tell the rest of Philadelphia that a man who can eat that
for supper doesn't need to be beholden to anyone."

But the most famous battle involving freedom of the
press erupted in New York, when a German immigrant
printer, John Peter Zenger, launched an attack on a corrupt
royal governor, William Cosby. Backed by a number of
wealthy Americans, Zenger began publishing the New York
Weekly Journal, four sheets that were crammed with gibes
at the governor and his friends. Here is how he described
one of the governor's stanchest supporters, the high
sheriff, a dumpy little man who liked to ride about in a
gorgeous red uniform on a prancing horse.

ADVERTISEMENT

A monkey of the largest sort, about four foot high, has
lately broke his chain and run into the country. . . . Having
got a warr saddle, pistols and sword, this whimsical creature
fancied himself a general; and taking a paper in his paw,
he muttered over it, what the far greatest part of the company understood not. . . .

Zenger soon had the whole town giving the governor the horselaugh. The governor did not think it was funny and after failing to persuade a grand jury to indict Zenger, Cosby took matters into his own hands and arrested the printer for criminal libel.

Zenger had courage. For nine months he languished in jail, but he continued to print his paper "through a hole in the wall." Actually his wife set the type and did much of the writing as well. Meanwhile, his friends did not desert him. When his case finally came to trial they retained for him the best-known lawyer of the time, Andrew Hamilton of Philadelphia.

Although he was over eighty, Hamilton yielded to the persuasions of his friend Ben Franklin and agreed to fight one more battle for liberty. He amazed the jury, and especially the judges, who were completely on the side of the governor, by admitting that Zenger had published the papers in question, and insisting that "the words themselves must be libelous, that is false, scandalous, and seditious, or else we are not guilty." This was a new idea in 1735. The law in those days maintained that if a newspaper attacked a politician in print, it was seditious libel; truth or falsehood had nothing to do with it.

When the judge pointed this out to Hamilton, he simply bowed and turned to the jury. "Then," he said, "it is to you we must now appeal." In a brilliant speech he evoked the deepest American emotions. "The question before the court and you, gentlemen of the jury, is not of small nor private concern; it is not the cause of the poor printer, nor of New York alone; no! it may in its consequence affect every free man that lives under a British government on the main of America. It is the best cause. It is the cause of liberty . . . the liberty both of exposing and opposing arbitrary power by speaking and writing Truth."

The jury brought back a verdict of "not guilty," and the courtroom burst into cheers.

2. FREEDOM GOES TOO FAR

It is hardly surprising, in the light of this history, to find Americans depending on their papers both for political news and political leadership throughout the Revolution. Ambrose Serle, a young Britisher who came over with the army to repress the rebellion, wrote home in 1776 about American newspapers. "One is astonished to see with what avidity they are sought after, and how implicitly they are believed, by the great bulk of the people. . . . Government [he meant British government] may find it expedient, in the sum of things, to employ this popular engine."

The British took his advice and backed some fifteen papers to sell their point of view during the long Revolutionary struggle. The most famous of these was James Rivington's *Royal Gazette*. Ceaselessly it pictured the patriot cause on the brink of military and financial collapse, libeled Washington and other American leaders by printing forged letters and reports of quarrels. Meanwhile, there is evidence that the wily Rivington was simultaneously spying for Washington.

Other newspapermen more than matched Rivington's

propaganda. The champion was, of course, English-born
Thomas Paine. On December 19, 1776, when the Revolutionary cause had sunk to its lowest ebb and Washington's
beaten army had skulked across the Delaware closely pursued by triumphant British grenadiers, the Pennsylvania
Journal published the first of a series of papers entitled
"The Crisis." Its opening sentences have become one of the
great documents of American history.

> These are the times that try men's souls. The Summer
> Soldier and the Sunshine Patriot will, in this crisis, shrink
> from the service of their country; but he that stands it now
> deserves the love and thanks of man and woman. Tyranny,
> like hell, is not easily conquered; yet we have this con-
> solation with us, that the harder the conflict, the more
> glorious the triumph. What we obtain too cheap, we esteem
> too lightly: it is dearness only that gives everything its
> value. Heaven knows how to put a proper price upon its
> goods; and it would be strange indeed if so celestial an
> article as FREEDOM should not be highly rated.

On December 24, while a desperate Washington was
planning to risk everything on a reckless raid across the
Delaware on the unlikely chance of surprising Hessian regi-
ments at Trenton, he read these words. The grim-eyed
American commander immediately ordered them read to
every regiment in his discouraged army. The next day
these ragged, half-frozen men fought like fiends at Trenton,
captured 900 Hessians and rescued the Revolution.

No wonder Washington was a stanch supporter of newspapers. When his army was quartered in Princeton during

the winter of 1777, he helped found the New Jersey *Gazette* to bolster his men's morale. Whenever tents or any other kind of cloth wore out, he ordered them sent to paper mills to be made into precious paper. Everywhere throughout the thirteen colonies, saving rags to make paper was considered a patriotic duty. The Massachusetts House of Representatives ordered local committees of safety to receive rags for the mills.

When politicians, generals and publishers all saw newspapers primarily as vehicles for publishing a particular point of view, they were only reflecting their readers. The one or two editors who tried to be impartial in the course of the Revolutionary struggle came close to getting hanged for their trouble. The most courageous of these was William Goddard, who with the help of his sister Mary published the Maryland *Gazette* in Baltimore. When he recommended that Americans accept peace terms that Great Britain offered in 1777, local patriots told him to close his paper and get out of town within forty-eight hours. The Maryland legislature came to Goddard's defense and he stayed in circulation. But two years later Goddard permitted Major General Charles Lee, second in command of the American army, to publish a slashing attack on George Washington in his pages. Lee had been court-martialed for insubordination at the battle of Monmouth and had become Washington's bitterest enemy. This time a well-armed mob marched on Goddard and at pistol point he was forced to write and publish a repudiation of Lee's attack. Only the presence of a few cooler heads saved Goddard from being hanged on the spot.

But Goddard was as stubborn as he was courageous.

Once more he appealed to the legislature and the moment he was assured of its protection he told off his persecutors and reaffirmed his determination to print his paper independently.

The war gave an enormous spurt to newspaper growth. It was no accident that when peace was finally declared and the American nation began its great experiment in freedom, the first daily paper was already on the street. It happened in Philadelphia, on May 30, 1783. Its name was the Pennsylvania *Evening Post and Daily Advertiser* and it was, according to one historian, "a sorry looking, poverty-stricken sheet," four pages long. The editor, Benjamin Towne, added still another innovation when he took to selling it on the street himself. "All the news for two coppers!" he howled. Business was brisk enough to inspire a rival paper, the Pennsylvania *Packet and Daily Advertiser,* to begin daily publication within a month. By the end of the century, Philadelphia had six dailies; New York, five; Baltimore, three; and Charleston, two. It was somehow fitting that with a new nation, a new era in newspapering was born.

But it was a somewhat superficial newness that American newspapers displayed. Daily or weekly, they all continued the tradition of highly personal political journalism. They were more interested in political views than news. Nothing and no one was sacred, and as the nation divided into two political parties—the conservative Federalist, led by Alexander Hamilton, and the liberal Republican, led by Thomas Jefferson—each group began financing papers and the nation soon had a literary donnybrook on its hands. Not even President Washington was exempt. Republican editor Benjamin Franklin Bache, grandson of old Ben, dared to declare: "If ever a nation was debauched by a man, the American nation has been debauched by Washington." When Washington retired at the end of his second term, Bache crowed: "This day ought to be a jubilee in the United States." He got as good as he gave from William Cobbett, who called himself Peter Porcupine and published *Porcupine's Gazette* for the Federalists. He cheered on hoodlums who beat up Bache in the streets and called his distinguished grandfather a "crafty and lecherous old hypocrite . . . whose very statue seems to gloat on the wenches as they walk the State House yard."

Significantly, none of these political papers made money and all went out of business the moment their patrons withdrew their support. Meanwhile, out of this welter of exaggeration and vituperation was emerging by slow degrees a new concept of a free press. In nine of the thirteen constitutions of the now independent United States, guarantees of freedom of the press were inserted. Oddly, the federal Constitution omitted any mention of it. But Thomas Jefferson and other brilliant Virginians, such as George Mason, fought fiercely for its inclusion in a Bill of Rights. At its first session, Congress bowed to these far-sighted lobbists and passed the ten amendments to the Constitution. The first one provided: "Congress shall make no law respecting an establishment of religion, or prohibiting the free exercise thereof; or of bridging the freedom of speech or of the press. . . ."

As Alexander Hamilton pointed out, liberty of the press was not easy to define. But he soon demonstrated to his great rival Jefferson that he too was capable of creating a landmark in the history of American journalism. Thus far, as we have seen, when a newspaper was sued for libel, the truth was not an issue in the case. In 1804, Hamilton defended Harry Croswell, editor of an obscure Hudson, New York, paper called *The Wasp*, who was arrested for libeling President Jefferson. As usual, the court refused to admit testimony as to the truth of the accusation. Hamilton took the case to the Supreme Court of the state of New York and in a brilliant speech argued that the press had "the right to publish with impunity, truth, with good motives, for justifiable ends, though reflecting on government, magistracy or individuals." Hamilton said this with relish, of course, because the "libel" he was defending was an attack on his chief rival. But he was so eloquent that the New York State Legislature soon passed a law making it possible to introduce the truth as the crucial issue in a libel suit.

Before the adoption of the Constitution, Jefferson had written, "Were it left to me to decide whether we should have a government without newspapers or newspapers without a government, I should not hesitate to prefer the latter." His fellow Americans watched him closely to see if he would change his mind when he became President, and the target of fierce newspaper attack. There were times he lost his temper and told one young man who planned to enter journalism, "Nothing can now be believed which is seen in a newspaper." But he gritted his teeth and stuck to his principles, in spite of abuse of the crudest, lowest sort. Jefferson was accused of seducing his slaves, of selling out America's interests for Napoleon's gold, of defrauding a widow of her estate when he was a young lawyer, and of attempting to seduce the wife of one of his best friends. One day, a distinguished visitor from Germany, the scientist Baron Alexander von Humboldt visited Jefferson, and while he was waiting in the President's study, began reading the newspapers, with some of these libels in them. Used to the European tradition, where the press was still severely regulated, the baron could not believe his eyes. When Jefferson came in, the German spluttered, "Why don't you have these scribblers jailed—or shot?"

Jefferson smiled and said, "When you go back to Europe, Baron, and they ask you about freedom in America, tell them about these papers, and where you found them."

Proudly, in the inaugural address opening his second term in the White House, Jefferson said: ". . . I have lent myself willingly as a subject of a great experiment, which was to prove that an administration conducting itself with integrity and common understanding cannot be battered down even by the falsehoods of a licentious press, and consequently still less by the press as restrained within the legal and wholesome limits of truth. . . . I have, therefore, never even contradicted the thousands of calumnies so industriously propagated against myself. But the fact being once established that the press is impotent when it abandons itself to falsehood, I leave to others to restore it to its strength by recalling it within the pale of truth."

This was precisely what began to happen. More and more thoughtful men began to realize that the real power of the press was its ability to print the truth about men and events. In Washington, D.C., a young journalist named Samuel Harrison Smith founded the first of the capital's great papers, the *National Intelligencer*. Socially as well as politically astute, Smith was a friend of Thomas Jefferson and entertained members of Congress lavishly. He soon became the semiofficial reporter of the House of Representatives and for over twenty-five years most papers in the United States depended on the *Intelligencer* to learn what was happening in the American capital. It was so different from the violently partisan papers of the day, one competitor nicknamed it "Mr. Silky Milky Smith's National Smoothing Plane."

But if the papers were improving, American readers had a way to go. When the *Federal Republican* in Baltimore published a protest against the War of 1812, a mob stormed the print shop, wrecked the presses and tore down the building. When Joseph M. Stret, editor of the *Western World* of Frankfort, Kentucky, exposed Aaron Burr's conspiracy to detach most of the Southwest from the United States and set up a private empire, numerous Kentuckians were enraged because he named them as Burr supporters. After fighting one duel, Stret announced that he had so many challenges he was going to file them "and from time to time give a list of them" in the paper.

Particularly in the West, editors had to be ready to defend their opinions with their lives if necessary. In the pre-Civil War decades, editors of the Vicksburg *Sentinel* had four men shot in duels or impromptu combat on the city's streets. Mark Twain began his career as a Western newspaperman and probably gave the best picture of this combative life in his famous sketch, "Journalism in Tennessee." In it the old editor, fresh from gunning one critic to earth, leaves some instructions for his new assistant.

Jones will be here at three—cowhide him. Gillespie will
call earlier, perhaps—throw him out of the window. Ferguson will be along about four—kill him. That is all for
today, I believe. If you have any odd time, you may
write a blistering article on the police. The cowhides are
under the table, weapons in the drawer, ammunition there
in the corner, lint and bandages up there in the pigeon-
holes. In case of accident, go to Lancet, the surgeon down-
stairs. He advertises; we take it out in trade.

Aaron Burr was one of the many politicians of the era
who had his own newspaper. He spent his time vilifying
Alexander Hamilton, who returned the abuse with interest
in his paper. The two men were soon enemies and when
Hamilton was in Albany defending Croswell, he made some
sneering remarks about Burr which got into the Albany
Register. Burr challenged Hamilton to a duel. They met a
few months later in Weehawken, New Jersey, and Burr
shot Hamilton dead.

Here is the story as written by Aaron Burr's paper, the
New York *Morning Chronicle:*

Colonel Burr arrived first on the ground as had been
previously agreed; when General Hamilton arrived the parties exchanged salutations and the seconds proceeded to
make their arrangements. They measured the distance, ten
full paces, and cast lots for the choice of position as also
to determine by whom the word should be given, both
of which fell to the second of General Hamilton. They
then proceeded to load the pistols in each other's presence,
after which the parties took their stations. The gentleman
who was to give the word then explained to the parties

the rules which were to govern them in firing, which were as follows:

"The parties being placed at their stations—the second who gives the word shall ask them whether they are ready; being answered in the affirmative he shall say, 'Present,' after this the parties shall present and fire when they please —if one fires before the other, the opposite second shall say, 'One, two, three, fire'—and shall then fire or lose his fire."

He then asked if they were prepared, being answered in the affirmative, he gave the word present, as had been agreed upon, and both parties took aim and fired in succession, the intervening time is not expressed, as the seconds do not agree on that point. The fire of Colonel Burr took effect, and General Hamilton almost instantly fell. Colonel Burr then advanced toward General Hamilton with a manner and gesture that appeared to General Hamilton's friend to be expressive of regret, but without speaking, turned about and withdrew, being urged from the field by his friend as has been subsequently stated, with a view to prevent his being recognized by the surgeon and barge man, who were then approaching. No further communication took place between the principals, and the barge that carried Colonel Burr immediately returned to the city. We conceive it proper to add that the conduct of the parties in this interview was perfectly proper, as suited the occasion.

Here is the story in Hamilton's *Evening Post:*

In the interviews that have since taken place between the gentlemen that were present, they have not been able to agree in two important facts that passed there—for which reason nothing was said on those subjects in the paper lately published as to other particulars in which they were agreed.

Mr. P(endleton) expressed a confident opinion that General Hamilton did not fire first—and that he did not fire at all at Colonel Burr. Mr. V(an) N(ess) seemed equally confident in opinion that General H did fire first—and of course that it must have been at his antagonist.

General Hamilton informed Mr. P at least ten days previous to the affair that he had doubts whether he would not receive and not return Mr. Burr's first fire. Mr. P remonstrated against this determination, and urged many considerations against it, as dangerous to himself and not necessary in the particular case, or on every ground of accommodation, not humiliating, had been proposed and rejected. He said he would not decide lightly, but take time to deliberate fully. It was incidentally mentioned again at their occasional subsequent conversations, and on the evening preceding the time of the appointed interview, he informed Mr. P he had made up his mind not to fire at Colonel Burr the first time, but to receive his fire, and fire in the air. Mr. P again urged him upon this subject and repeated his former arguments. His final answer was in terms that made an impression on Mr. P's mind which can never be effaced. "My friend, it is the effect of a religious scruple, and does not admit of reasoning; it is useless to say more on the subject, as my purpose is definitely fixed."

His last words before he was wounded afford a proof that his purpose had not changed. When he received his pistol, after having taken his position, he was asked if he would have the hairspring set. His answer was, "Not this time."

After he was wounded, and laid in the boat, the first words he uttered after recovering his power of speech were (addressing himself to a gentleman present who perfectly

well remembers it) "Pendleton knows I did not mean to
fire at Colonel Burr the first time."

The pistol had been used by General Hamilton, laying
loose over the other apparatus in the case which was opened;
after having been some time in the boat, one of the boat-
men took hold of it, to put it in the case. General Hamilton
observing this said, "Take care of the pistol—it is cocked.
It may go off and do mischief." This is also remembered by
the gentleman alluded to.

This shows he was not sensible of having fired at all.
If he had fired previous to receiving the wound, he would
have remembered it, and therefore have known that the
pistol could not go off; but if afterwards it must have been
the effect of an involuntary exertion of the muscles produced
by a mortal wound, in which case he would not have been
conscious of having fired.

Mr. P having so strong a conviction that if General
Hamilton had fired first, it could not have escaped his
attention (all his anxiety being alive for the effect of the
first fire and having no reason to believe the friend of
Colonel Burr was not sincere in the contrary opinion) he
determined to go to the spot where the affair took place,
to see if he could not discover some traces of the course
of the ball from General Hamilton's pistol. He took a
friend with him the day after General Hamilton died, and
after some examination they fortunately found what they
were in search of. They ascertained that the ball passed
through the limb of a cedar tree, at an elevation of about 12
feet and an half, perpendicularly from the ground, between
13 and 14 feet from the mark on which General Hamilton
stood, and about 4 feet wide of the direct line between
him and Colonel Burr, on the right side; he having fallen
on the left. The part of the limb through which the ball

passed was cut off and brought to the city, and is now in Mr. Church's possession.

No inferences are pointed out as resulting from these facts, nor will any comments be made. They are left to the candid judgement and feelings of the public.

The *Evening Post* published additional stories about the duel, which had not a little to do with influencing a coroner's inquest to find that "Aaron Burr, Esquire, Vice President of the United States, was guilty of the murder of Alexander Hamilton." Burr had to flee New York State and thereafter his political career slid dismally downhill, until he tried to lead a revolution against Jefferson's administration, only to be exposed by, among others, the editor of the *Western World*.

Newspapers continued to grow. Wherever Americans went there was almost certain to be one hardy fellow who managed to pack a printing press. By 1820, there were 512 newspapers being published in the United States, 24 dailies, 66 semiweeklies and 422 weeklies. In 1828 came a new role for the newspaperman: adviser to a President.

The man was Francis P. Blair, the President, Andrew Jackson. A tall, cadaverous individual described by a friend as "when dressed in thick winter clothing, 107 pounds all told," Blair was a Kentuckian, whose paper, *The Argus of Western America,* was one of the few that supported Jackson in his rugged battle for the presidency. No sooner was Jackson in the White House than he ordered Blair to head for Washington where he swiftly established him as the editor of a new paper, the Washington *Globe.* "Send it to Bla-ar," became Jackson's favorite solution whenever he

was confronted with a baffling problem. Two fellow editors
on the *Argus* came with Blair and together they formed
what was soon called "the Kitchen Cabinet." The three
newspapermen were with Jackson at all hours of the day
and night. "Old Hickory" would lie on a couch smoking
and dictating his ideas to the scholar of the group, Amos
Kendall. Blair would then rewrite the stuff into whiplash
editorials at a speed that kept two copy boys running the
paragraphs to the typesetters.

Soon everyone in the world was reading the *Globe*, to
find out what was going on inside the Jackson administration. Ambassadors abroad protested in vain that the paper
did not represent the official policy of the United States
Government. As with *Pravda* today, when a politician's
name was studiously omitted from the *Globe*'s pages for
weeks at a time, everyone knew that the bottom had
dropped out of his White House stock. Soon Blair was
boasting to his sister-in-law of his influence with Jackson.
"Where I am I can do nothing wrong. If Van Buren
[Martin Van Buren, then political boss of the state of New
York] says, 'You are rash in this business, Mr. Blair,'
the old hero says, 'You are right, Mr. Blair, I'll stand by
you.'" Backed by Jackson, Blair was a formidable antagonist. He destroyed John C. Calhoun as presidential candidate
and then proceeded to do an equally savage wrecking job
on Henry Clay. His sarcasm, in the words of one historian,
"bit like vipers." He was also an empire builder and any
newspaperman that shifted to a pro-Jackson position was
almost certain to get a good job with the government.

But the slow, almost invisible, growth of a spirit of
independence in the newspaper profession continued. In

1832, the *National Intelligencer* published a list of fifty-seven journalists who had been handed federal appointments by Jackson. The Richmond *Inquirer,* which had backed Jackson stanchly for re-election, complained, "We wish the executive would let the press alone."

This statement was a sign of a distinct shift in mood among newspapermen. Little by little, they were beginning to realize that they did not need the backing of a politician or a political party to succeed. Thanks to a series of important new inventions, a genuinely new era in American newspapering was about to begin.

3. FIRST OF THE GIANTS

The revolution began in New York, with a new idea: cheap news. Heretofore, papers were expensive—a yearly subscription cost $8 to $10, a full week's wages for a skilled worker; the equivalent in modern cash would be about $100. As a result, papers were bought (but not exclusively read) by members of the upper class and circulation was small—about 1500 on the average. But the number of papers continued to grow at a fantastic rate. By 1833, there were three times as many newspapers in the United States as in England or in France. Shrewd, thoughtful men surveying the American passion for newspapers began plotting ways of selling news cheaper and better. They had on their side the industrial revolution and its perpetual search for better and better machinery. The arrival of new, fast steam-driven presses in the 1830s was the signal for the news revolution to begin.

At its head were two totally different New York newspapermen, James Gordon Bennett and Horace Greeley. Both saw the possibility of publishing newspapers for the man in the street, charging as little as a penny a copy and making a profit on the thousands of pennies mass circulation could capture.

Bennett was by far the more flamboyant. "Shakespeare is the great genius of the drama," he wrote, "Scott of the novel, Milton and Byron of the poem—and I mean to be the genius of the newpaper press." He swiftly proved he had the stuff to back up his ambition. One of the great iconoclasts, he had no respect for anybody, simply because he happened to have a formidable title or an exaggerated claim to expertise. With $500 in his pocket, Bennett set himself up in a Wall Street cellar with an ailing press and a desk made of a plank laid across two flour barrels. Out of this hole in the ground appeared a newspaper called the New York *Herald*. In fifteen months, he had a circulation of 40,000 and was able to boldly raise his price to two cents a copy.

Bennett was not only a great editor and reporter—he was the first philosopher of the newspaper business. "An editor must always be with the people—think with them— feel with them—and he need fear nothing, he will always be right, always be strong—always popular—always free. The world has been humbugged long enough by spouters and talkers and conventioners and legislators. . . . This is the editorial age."

He boldly opted for realism, ignoring the complaints of the puritanical, printing *legs* for *limbs* and *shirt* for *linen* and *trousers* for *unmentionables*. "What is to prevent a daily newspaper from being made the greatest organ of social life?" he asked his readers. "Books have had their day—the theaters have had their day—the temple of religion has had its day. A newspaper can be made to take the

lead of all these in the great movements of human thought
and of human civilization. A newspaper can send more
souls to heaven and save more from hell than all the
churches or chapels in New York—besides making money
at the same time. Let it be tried."

There are so many firsts connected with Bennett's name,
the list almost grows tedious. He was the first newspaperman to do a genuine reporting job on a murder story.
When Helen Jewett, a prostitute, was found murdered in
her room, a young clerk named Robinson was arrested
and his guilt was considered a foregone conclusion. Bennett
himself investigated the case and blasted police and politicians in his paper, defending Robinson's innocence. He
covered the trial day by day, word by word, printing
verbatim testimony that tripled his circulation and shocked
more sedate New Yorkers out of their socks.

Bennett also reported society news, always with a touch
of satire. Above all, the people loved the way Bennett
dramatized himself and told the truth with total frankness.
When one of his editorial enemies assaulted him on the
street, knocking him flat with a cudgel and cutting open
his head, Bennett wrote: "The fellow no doubt wanted
to let out the never-failing supply of good humor and wit
which has created such a reputation for the *Herald,* and
appropriate the contents to supply the emptiness of his own
thick skull." When he raised the price of the *Herald,* he
published a complete financial statement showing his readers how much he proposed to earn from the increase
($999.96 a week). "With this sum," he wrote, "I shall be
enabled to carry into effect prodigious improvements and

to make the *Herald* the greatest, best and most profitable paper that ever appeared in this country."

While he was winning the man in the street, Bennett made enemies by the dozen. This 1836 editorial, which also gives a good picture of how he operated, explains why.

We published yesterday the principal items of the foreign news received by the Sheffield, being eight days later than our previous arrivals. Neither the *Sun* nor the *Transcript* had a single item on the subject. The *Sun* did not even know of its existence. The large papers in Wall Street had also the news, but as the editors are lazy, ignorant, indolent, blustering blockheads, one and all, they did not pick out the cream and serve it as we did. The *Herald* alone knows how to dish up foreign news, or indeed domestic news, in a readable style. Every reader, numbering between 30 and 40 thousand *daily*, acknowledges this merit in the management of our paper. We do not, as the Wall Street lazy editors do, come down to our office about 10 or 12 o'clock, pull out a Spanish cigar, pick up a pair of scissors, puff and cut, cut and puff for a couple of hours and then adjourn to Delmonico's to eat, drink, gormandize, and blow up our contemporaries. We arise in the morning at 5:00, write our leading editorials, squibs, sketches, etc., before breakfast. From nine to one we read all our papers and original communications, the latter being more numerous than those of any other office in New York. From these we pick out facts, thoughts, hints and incidents sufficient to make up a column of original spicy articles. We also give audiences to visitors, gentlemen on business and some of the loveliest ladies in New York, who call to subscribe—Heaven bless them! At one we sally out among the gentlemen and loafers of Wall Street—and find out the state of the money market, return, finish the next day's paper—close every piece of business requiring thought, sentiment, feeling or philosophy before four o'clock. We then dine moderately and temperately—read our proofs—take in cash and advertisements which are increasing like smoke—and close the day always by going to bed at 10 o'clock, seldom later. That's the way to conduct a paper with spirit and success.

In no time at all, the so-called best people in New York were arrayed almost 100 per cent in a "moral war" on Bennett and the *Herald*. But Bennett went coolly forward, creating more firsts. He set up a European bureau and a Washington bureau and sent reporters out to cover regular "beats" around New York. When the proprietors of the Astor House refused to admit Bennett and his bride, Bennett cheerfully replied, "These blockheads are determined to make me the greatest man of the age. Newspaper abuse made Mr. Van Buren chief magistrate of this republic—and newspaper abuse will make me the chief editor of this country. Well—be it so, I can't help it."

For all his brilliance, Bennett never achieved the political influence of his great rival, Horace Greeley. If Bennett was the man who showed newspapermen how to make their profession part of the meat and drink of daily life for the average man, Greeley demonstrated a newspaper's power for moral leadership. A New England farm boy who came to New York with bumpkin written all over him, he built his paper, the *Tribune,* into a national voice with his intense concern for moral issues. He never stopped talking and more than a few people thought he was out of his mind.

But "Uncle Horace," as he was affectionately known, had a unique ability to stir the heart of the average man, where Bennett titillated his interest.

Beginning in 1841, six years after the *Herald,* Greeley never caught Bennett in the circulation race. But his *Weekly Tribune,* a condensation of the daily paper, was mailed throughout the United States. "The *Tribune* comes next to the Bible all through the West," was soon an American truism. This faith sprang from clear-cut evidence that Horace Greeley meant it when he said the purpose of his "new morning journal of politics, literature and general intelligence" was to "advance the interest of the people and promote their moral, political and social well-being." By 1860, the weekly edition had attained a record-breaking circulation of 200,000.

Greeley pursued causes with tireless passion. He never said, "Go West, young man, go West," a remark which was frequently attributed to him. But he did campaign to convince the poor in the overcrowded cities of the East that there was opportunity on the border. Interviewing Brigham Young on a western tour of his own, Greeley came back to attack Mormon polygamy so violently that it was outlawed three years later. He campaigned with equal vigor against capital punishment and persuaded several state governments to abolish the hangman's noose. But his two overwhelming concerns were the working man and the abolition of slavery. "The great, the all-embracing reform of our age," said Greeley in a lecture, "is the social reform—that which seeks to lift the laboring class as such—not out of labor, by any means—but out of ignorance, inefficiency, dependence, and want."

Against slavery Greeley was a fearless campaigner. He sent reporters into the South to tell in graphic detail what happened at slave auctions. Here is how one of Greeley's men reported a dialogue between a slave and a would-be buyer.

Alicia, chattel No. 5 in the catalogue, had taken a fancy to a benevolent looking middle aged gentleman who was inspecting the stock, and thus used his powers of persuasion to induce the benevolent man to purchase him with his wife, boy and girl, Molly, Israel and Sevanda, chattels No. 6, 7 and 8.

"Look at me, mas'er. Am prime rice planter; sho' you won't find a better man den me; no better on de whole plantation; not a bit old yet. Do mo' work den ever. Do carpenter work, too, little. Better buy me, mas'er. I'se be good sarvent, mas'er. Molly, too, my wife, suh. Fus' rate rice hands; mos' as good as me. Stan' out yer, Molly, and let the gen'lem'n see."

Molly advances, with her hands crossed on her bosom, and makes a quick curtsy, and stands mute, looking appealingly in the benevolent man's face. But Alicia talks all the faster.

"Show mas'er your arm, Molly—good arm dat, mas'er. She do a heap of work mo' with dat arm yet. Let good mas'er see your teeth, Molly—see dat, mas'er. Teeth all reg'lar. All good. She's young gal yet. Come out yer, Israel. Walk aroun' an' let the gen'lem'n see how spry you be."

Then pointing to the three year old girl who stood with her chubby hand to her mouth, holding onto her mother's dress, and uncertain what to make of the strange scene;

"Little Vandy's on'y a chile yet; make prime gal by-and-

by. Better buy us, mas'er. We'm fus'-rate bargain"—and
so on.

But the benevolent gentleman found where he could
drive a closer bargain and so bought somebody else.

Greeley and Bennett did not entirely dominate the New
York scene. They had a formidable rival in a paper called
The Sun, which was run by a succession of managers. It
achieved its greatest notoriety with a stunt that sent its
circulation soaring to hitherto undreamt-of heights, the
largest—at the time—of any newspaper in the world. In
August 1835, the paper printed a short paragraph about
"astronomical discoveries of the most wonderful description," which had just been made by Sir John Herschel, son
of the discoverer of the planet Uranus. A few days later *The
Sun's* first page trumpeted an announcement of still more
discoveries, supposedly copied from the *Edinburgh Journal
of Science.* Thanks to a new telescope, the writer declared
that Sir John had discovered planets and other solar systems
and had been able to study the moon with a clarity "fully
equal to that which the unaided eye commands of terres-
trial objects at the distance of 100 yards." The next day
the series continued with a discussion of flora and fauna
on the moon, including a description of a "strange am-
phibious creature of a spherical form which rolled with
great velocity across the pebbly beach." Papers around the
nation hastily reprinted the story and were even more
goggle-eyed by its successors which described moonmen.
Yale University dispatched a delegation to New York to
investigate. Requests for pamphlets and pictures poured in
from around the world.

The next day the reporter who was writing the series confided to a drinking friend that the whole thing was a hoax. The friend happened to be a fellow reporter and the news was soon on the streets. *The Sun* coolly admitted the deception, and even tried to take some credit for it, claiming it had succeeded in "diverting the public mind for a while from that bitter apple of discord, the abolition of slavery."

But a hoax a week could not have managed this miracle. From New York where Bennett crossed editorial swords with Greeley over the issue, newspapers throughout the nation engaged in furious debate over a mounting antagonism between North and South. More than once readers expressed their opinions with typically American direct action. John Greenleaf Whittier's Pennsylvania *Freeman*, published in Philadelphia, was wrecked by a mob in 1838 for its Abolitionist views. Another anti-slavery paper, the *Philanthropist*, was wrecked three times in Cincinnati during the late 1830s. A tragic climax to these violent reactions was the murder of the Reverend Elijah P. Lovejoy, editor of the *Observer*. Driven out of St. Louis by hostile readers, he moved across the river to Alton, Illinois. There, three times in one year his press was seized and flung into the Mississippi. But Lovejoy was tough. He ordered a fourth press; as he was setting it up another mob attacked and all-out war erupted. A pistol shot killed Lovejoy instantly and he became one of the best-known martyrs of the Abolitionist crusade.

But newspapers continued to grow in number and size. Although the New York press dominated the nation for a while, once the telegraph linked the cities and towns, it was no longer necessary to wait for New York papers to arrive by train or steamboat. The American passion for public education was also an important factor in making the United States a nation of readers. By 1860, illiteracy had declined to a mere 9 per cent of the population. No matter where Americans went, newspapers went with them. By 1860, there were no less than one hundred in California alone. Chicago had eleven dailies and twenty-two weeklies. It was the editor of the Chicago *Tribune,* Joseph Medill, who built up a nationwide boom for an Illinois politician named Abraham Lincoln. With Lincoln's election the stage was set for a great national drama, in which newspapers would play a unique role.

4. THE REPORTER'S WAR

On April 12, 1861, James Gordon Bennett was hard at work making the New York *Herald* "the greatest, best and most profitable paper that ever appeared." Suddenly, into his office dashed a breathless messenger from the telegraph office. The wire was from Charleston, South Carolina, and the man who sent it was a *Herald* reporter named Felix Gregory De Fontaine. Bennett took one look at it and began roaring orders for a special edition.

The message read:

> Civil war has at last begun. A terrible fight is at this moment going on between Fort Sumter and the fortifications by which it is surrounded. . . .
>
> The excitement in the community is indescribable. With the first boom of the gun, thousands rushed from their beds to the harbor front and all day every available place has been thronged by ladies and gentlemen, viewing the solemn spectacle through their glasses. Most of these have relatives in the several fortifications, and many a tearful eye attests to the anxious affection of the mother, wife and sister, but not a murmur came from a single individual. . . . The

thunder of the artillery can be heard for fifty miles around. . . .

It was the scoop of the century. No other reporter was able to get the story out so quickly and in such detail. Other papers had reporters in Charleston, where tension between the Federal troops in Fort Sumter and the defiant Southerners had been mounting for weeks. But when the firing started, local authorities hastily jailed almost every reporter but Fontaine—and permitted only him to use the telegraph. With a shrewdness worthy of his boss, Fontaine had become a good friend of the Southern commanding general, Pierre Beauregard.

On the following day, Fort Sumter surrendered, and the *Herald* sold an astonishing 135,600 copies. Bennett being Bennett, he did not hesitate to point out that this was the largest single issue in newspaper history. New Yorkers were so eager to get the news, police had to surround the Herald building, and take steps to prevent a riot.

Other papers rushed to overtake the *Herald*'s head start in covering the war. Henry Raymond, the publisher of the New York *Times,* turned himself into a combat reporter. Horace Greeley, Bennett's rival on the New York *Tribune,* tried to hire prominent Washington politicians to get inside news of the government's decisions. But Bennett was equally determined to stay ahead. He rushed no less than forty correspondents to the fighting fronts. The Civil War was on its way to becoming history's best-reported war.

The Bohemian Brigade, as the reporters called themselves, swiftly evolved a new technique for getting the truth about the war to their readers. Samuel Wilkeson of the *Tribune* summed it up: "The only way to report battles

was by being so closely observant of them as to be in
danger of being killed." Soon numerous army men were
talking about the bravery of reporters under fire. Sometimes
they even participated in the fighting. At the battle of
Antietam, Major General Joseph Hooker was wounded by
a Confederate sharpshooter early in the day. He converted
George Smalley into a dispatch rider, and again and again
Smalley rushed from Hooker's bedside to deliver crucial
orders through swarms of Confederate bullets. Before the
day was over he had two bullets through his clothes and
another had killed his horse.

The exhausted fighting men could at least sleep beside
their guns. But Smalley's job had only begun. He rode all
night to reach a telegraph office thirty miles away. But the
wire went to the War Department, and the bureaucrats
there sat on it, refusing to forward the news to his paper in
New York. Smalley wangled his way on board a government train and got to Baltimore. There he leaped aboard a
New York express and stayed up for the second consecutive
night, writing his story beneath a single swaying oil lamp.
"I ended as the train rolled into Jersey City by daylight,"
he recalled. By breakfast time, the *Tribune* was on the
street with six columns of Smalley's eyewitness description
of "the greatest fight since Waterloo."

Such intimate familiarity with the fighting front often
enabled reporters to make devastating criticisms of some
generals' military tactics. At Fredericksburg, Oswald Garrison Villard crouched in a ditch, close enough to hear the
cries of the wounded and the dying as wave after wave of
Federal soldiers launched doomed assaults on Robert E.
Lee's Southern army, entrenched in the heights around the

town. Hoping to soften the news of the catastrophe, the Union general, Ambrose Burnside, refused to allow anyone to use either the mail or the telegraph. Villard rowed out to a boat in the Potomac River and talked the captain into taking him to Washington. His story infuriated the nation, and Burnside was fired a few weeks later.

Another reporter made the mistake of suggesting that William Tecumseh Sherman was insane. He had been led astray by Sherman's excitable, talkative personality. The experience converted Sherman into a fierce foe of all reporters. He maintained that they were all potential spies. When a Bohemian was so foolish as to ask Sherman for a pass, which would let him wander from unit to unit throughout the army, "Uncle Billy" growled, "You have two hours to get out of this department, or I'll hang you." A few months later, an aide rushed into Sherman's tent and told him that three reporters had been killed by a shell. "Good," snarled the general, "we'll have some news from hell before breakfast." This ferocious antagonism inclined some reporters to criticize Sherman unjustly. But many others ignored his blistering tongue and recognized him for the great general that he was.

The risks which some reporters took were almost incredible. Albert B. Richardson of the New York *Tribune* watched the bombardment of Fort Henry from the top of a tall tree which stood between the Federal gunboats and the fort. With another *Tribune* reporter, he attempted to run the Confederate blockade at Vicksburg in a small unarmed tug. Southern batteries all but blew it out of the water, killing the captain, exploding the boiler and sending the two reporters and the crew leaping into the Mississippi with flames all around them. Captured, they were sent to various military prisons in the South, finally escaped and trudged through North Carolina into Tennessee in mid-winter, hiding by night, wading streams up to their waists in icy water, dodging Southern patrols until they stumbled into Knoxville more dead than alive. Richardson, true to his reporter's credo, rushed to the telegraph office to wire his story to the *Tribune*. "Out of the jaws of death," it began, "out of the mouth of hell."

Not all the Bohemians served on land. The Civil War was also a naval conflict, and the man who covered that side of the war better than any other reporter was B. S. Osbon of the *Herald*. Osbon, whose name was often mis-spelled as Osborn, was aboard the little revenue cutter *Harriet Lane,* standing off Fort Sumter when the Con-federate gunners fired the first shot of the war. He got the story of the fort's brief struggle and final capitulation from the commander, Major Robert Anderson, himself. Perhaps because he had spent much of his life at sea, Osbon got a roving commission from the Secretary of War to "ac-company naval expeditions in any staff capacity to which the commanders might appoint him." With this for an open-ing wedge, he persuaded Admiral David Farragut to ap-point him as his signal officer. He thus occupied a central role in one of the great dramas of the war—the conquest of New Orleans. It was he who gave the signals to the Union fleet to attack the city. It meant running the gantlet of two huge forts mounting two hundred guns, plus a chain barrier through which a very narrow opening had been cleared. After that came a dozen or so Confederate gunboats, and countless fire rafts. No one can improve on Osbon's version of the story.

"It was a solemn time. On the stroke of two with my own hands I hoisted to the mizzen peak a pair of red lanterns which was the signal to get under way. The first ship was just at the chain when a blaze of light and a roar from the fort told we had been discovered. Shells and shot screamed through the rigging as the ships crowded through the opening." Osbon boldly hoisted "the largest Star Spangled Banner at the peak and decked the fore and main masts in the same way." The situation soon became totally chaotic, as the ships dueled to the death with the guns in the forts. Osbon described Farragut's sailors, with their powder-blackened faces, as looking "like a lot of demons in a wild inferno." Meanwhile, above the battle stood the indomitable Farragut. He had climbed high in the mizzen rigging so he could see above the powder smoke. "With his feet on the ratlines and his back against the shrouds, he stood there as cool and undisturbed as if leaning against a mantel in his own home," Osbon wrote. Several times Osbon climbed up through the whirring shells to take orders from him. Then he noticed that the cannon balls were coming closer and closer. He begged Farragut to come down. The admiral had barely placed his feet on the deck when a shell exploded where he had been standing, shredding the ratlines and rigging.

At 4:15 A.M., while the flagship's batteries continued to duel with the forts, she went aground. At the same moment a Confederate ship called the *Ram* (designed to ram and sink enemy ships) shoved a fire raft under the flagship. Farragut, rushing to put out the flames before they blew up his ship, saw Osbon on his knees. "Come, sir, this is no time for prayer," the admiral shouted. He soon found out that the reporter was busy uncapping some twenty-pound shells which he threw over the side into the fire raft. They exploded almost instantly and the raft sank. The *Herald*'s reporter had saved the admiral and his flagship.

Not long after, when Farragut sent dispatches to Washington, he let Osbon accompany them, on the small cutter. As the dispatch boat left the flagship, the sailors manned the rigging and gave the reporter three mighty cheers, and as the small boat went down the river, every ship in the fleet paid Osbon the same compliment. A few days later, the reporter gave President Lincoln a personal report on the capture of New Orleans and rushed to New York to deliver his story to the *Herald*. It was a tremendous scoop. He had been the only reporter aboard Farragut's fleet.

Newspapers were read with equal fervor in the South, during the war. The Southerners organized a Press Association which sent news to forty-three daily papers. In the best tradition of American journalism, they told the truth, even when the news was bad. "PA," as the association was called, was often quoted by Northern papers—perhaps the best proof of its reliability. But as with General Sherman, reporters were sometimes inclined to make snap judgments about the talents of some generals. Early in the war, Robert E. Lee was forced to abandon western Virginia in the face of superior Union forces. Reporters denounced him in the Richmond papers as "Granny" Lee. Although Confederate President Jefferson Davis knew that Lee was probably the best general he had, for some months he hesitated to give him command of the main army.

With the Northern navy blockading their ports, and Northern armies invading their territory, Southern papers sometimes had difficulty staying in business. There were constant shortages of paper, ink, editors and printers, not to mention the threat of imminent capture. Frank Luther Mott, the best-known historian of American journalism, obviously admired the odyssey of the Memphis *Appeal*, which departed from Tennessee one jump ahead of the Union armies in June 1862.

Loaded on a flat car, its press and type were taken successively to the Mississippi towns of Hernando, Vicksburg and Grenada, in each of which it continued to publish; always routed out by the approach of Grant or Sherman, it gained the nickname of the Moving Appeal. It was forced from its next refuge, Jackson, Mississippi, by shellfire announcing the indomitable Sherman; and it crossed Pearl River while the shells dropped around the press. On the Southern Railroad it fled to Meridian and thence to Atlanta, where it was issued for over a year. The paper got out of that city just before Sherman marched in. It was published thereafter in Montgomery, Alabama, and three other Georgia towns, finding itself at last by a perverse fate once more squarely in the path of Sherman's march to the sea. Despairing, its editor, Colonel Benjamin Franklin Dill, loaded a proof press on a mule's back, put some type in his saddlebags and took to the mountains—where bluecoats finally caught up with him at Columbus, Georgia, and ended his odyssey. . . . The *Appeal* had been published in ten towns and four states.

Not even personal tragedy stopped reporters from doing their jobs. Sam Wilkeson's nineteen-year-old son was killed in the first day's fighting at Gettysburg. Sitting beside the boy's open grave, the weeping father wrote a vivid description of the climactic battle and sent it to his paper.

After two years of war, most Bohemians were cool professionals at Gettysburg. Francis Grey told his *Tribune* readers, "Matters do not look particularly encouraging here. The Rebels seem to be on all sides. At present I am under a knoll writing this with a perfect shower of rifle balls and shells passing over." When Confederate artillery opened a furious bombardment of Cemetery Hill, several reporters sat boldly in the open near General Meade's headquarters, arguing about the best way to describe the howls and whizzes of the shells that were exploding all around them.

A New York *World* reporter wrote:

> The boards of fences, scattered by explosions, flew in splinters through the air. The earth torn up in clouds blinded the eyes of hurrying men. . . . As with hundreds of others I groped through this tempest of death to the shelter of a bluff, an old man, a private in a company belonging to the 24th Michigan, was struck scarcely ten feet away by a cannon ball which tore through him, extorting such a low, intense cry of mortal pain as I pray God I may never hear again.

Standing on Cemetery Hill, Whitelaw Reid of the Cincinnati *Gazette* reported how Pickett's charge looked eyeball-to-eyeball.

> . . . They were in point blank range. At last the order came! From thrice six thousand guns there came a sheet

of smoky flame, a crash of leaden death. The line literally melted away; but there came the second resistless still. . . . Up to the rifle pits and across them, over the barricades, the momentum of their charge, the mere machine strength of their combined action, swept them on. . . .

The last murderous guns were still booming at Gettysburg when Homer Byington of the *Tribune* rushed to the telegraph office to send his story to New York. Glumly he was informed that the line was dead. Southern cavalrymen had cut it. Flashing a fistful of bills, Byington persuaded a crew of telegraph repairmen to string five miles of new wire. Back to the office rushed Byington to flash his story to New York. It was a clean beat and the *Tribune* sold 65,000 copies of a night extra. Bells rang and horns sounded as the city went mad with joy. Byington also flashed a wire to Washington, informing it that trains were badly needed for the wounded. Washington replied that the trains would be sent at once. The message was signed "A. Lincoln." Once more, a reporter had gotten news of a crucial battle to the harried President, while his generals were hesitating to wire him.

Henry A. Wing, a cub reporter for the *Tribune*, did more than send Lincoln a wire. He carried a personal message from Ulysses S. Grant, the Union commander in chief, to the desperately anxious President from the confused, chaotic battlefield called The Wilderness. Grant was trying to break through to Richmond in an all-out effort to end the war. The first two days' fighting ended in a bloody stalemate. Wing and several other *Tribune* reporters gathered for a conference and decided one of them should

ride back to Washington with the news. Wing was selected.
It was a dangerous assignment. Confederate guerrillas and
squadrons of roaming Southern cavalry infested the roads.
"You expect to get through to Washington?" Ulysses Grant
asked the twenty-four-year-old Connecticut ex-soldier.

Wing said he was going to try. "Well, if you see the
President," Grant said, "tell him for me that whatever
happens there will be no turning back."

Wing began his journey wearing the more or less official
uniform of a *Tribune* correspondent—corduroy knickers, a
buckskin jacket and expensive leather boots. But at Cul-
pepper, Virginia, a friend advised him to abandon this
handsome outfit, and disguise himself as a field hand. So
Wing put on an old shirt, a pair of dirty trousers, some
muddy shoes and a battered cap. "Make believe you're a
Southerner, on your way to Washington to tell some Rebel
friends that Lee has beaten Grant and is on his way to
the capital," the friend advised Wing.

Wing had ridden only a few miles when he found himself staring down the wrong end of a Confederate pistol.
He faked a Southern accent, and told them his phony
story. The Southerners were so convinced, they gave him
an escort to make sure he wasn't captured by Union patrols.
But at Kelly's Ford, on the Rappahannock, Wing's luck
ran out. Kelly was a dedicated secessionist, and he instantly recognized Wing. "Grab him, he's a Yankee," he
roared. Wing dug his spurs into his horse and leaped into
the swift-running river. Horse and rider escaped a hail of
shots and reached the other side. On Wing rode, talking
his way through several more Confederate outposts. But he
finally decided it was only a matter of time before his luck

would fail him permanently. He was simply too conspicuous on horseback. He tied the horse in a thicket, left him the bag of oats, and started hiking to Washington along the rail line. After several hours of weary walking, he found himself captured by another Confederate cavalry unit. The commander suspected Wing was a spy and when the reporter drawled out the story of Lee's victory, he was told that they would see the word got to Washington. Curtly, he ordered Wing put under guard.

Fortunately, the guards were careless, and as soon as it grew dark, Wing was able to slip into the night. Several more hours of walking finally brought him to the Union lines once more. Spotting a railroad handcar nearby, he tried to bribe some soldiers into letting him use it. He was told the army had taken over the railroad. Then he heard the welcome chatter of a telegraph. He rushed into the shack and begged for permission to use it. After a great deal of arguing, the officer in charge agreed to ask Secretary of War Stanton to let Wing send a one-hundred-word report to his paper.

Stanton did not like reporters. He felt they gave away valuable military secrets with their mania for getting the facts. Back from the War Department in Washington came a sharp reply: "Send your news from Grant immediately. Otherwise we'll have you arrested as a spy."

Wing refused. "The *Tribune* comes first," he insisted.

Wing was close to despair. He had no sleep since 4 A.M. the previous morning and had walked twenty-four miles on a leg that had been badly wounded at Fredericksburg. Then the telegraph chattered again. A goggle-eyed clerk handed Wing the message.

This is the President. Mr. Stanton tells me you have news from the army. Will you give it to me? We are anxious here in Washington to learn developments at the front.

For a moment Wing was staggered. He realized that Grant, still absorbed in the battle, had sent no news. Although he sympathized with the President, Wing did not forget he was a newspaperman.

Mr. Lincoln: I am sorry to cause you anxiety but my news is for the *Tribune*. I will be glad to tell you all I know if you will see that a message goes forward tonight to my paper. I left Grant's headquarters at 4 this morning.

Back came the reply:

Of course; if you'll entrust your report to me I will see that it goes to the *Tribune*.

A few hours later, Wing was dozing on a bench when a special train came chugging down from Washington, by order of the President. An hour later, he was hustled into the White House to confront not only the President, but Secretary of War Stanton and all the other members of the Cabinet. They listened to his description of the bitter two-day battle. But they were obviously disappointed that he did not bring them news of a great Union victory. Wing waited until the Cabinet members left, and then he asked the President if he could speak to him alone. The President looked baffled, then nodded. When Lincoln heard Grant's message, a glow of joy illuminated his face. So many other

Union generals had retreated to Washington after their first collision with Robert E. Lee. Now the President knew that he had finally found a general who would fight to the finish. To Wing's amazement, the haggard but happy President put his arm around the cub reporter and kissed him on the cheek.

Wing stumbled to a room at the National Hotel and collapsed into a deep sleep without even bothering to take off his muddy clothes. Hours later, shouts of newsboys in the streets below awakened him. "EXTRA, EXTRA," they called. "NEWS FROM THE ARMY. GRANT FOUND." Dazedly, Wing realized that it was his own story they were selling.

Later that day, Wing went back to the White House for another talk with Lincoln. After describing the fighting in more detail, he told the President the story of his journey from the battlefield. He told Lincoln he deeply regretted having had to abandon his horse, Jess. The horse was so intelligent and good-natured, he regarded him as a personal friend. Lincoln, a fellow horse lover, equipped Wing with a special train and a squad of soldiers and sent him down the railroad to the thicket where he had left Jess. There stood the good horse, still waiting for his master, forty-eight hours later. Wing coaxed him aboard the train and sped him back to Washington. Thereafter there was a special bond between Wing and Lincoln. Whenever he returned to Washington, he gave the President a personal report on the army's morale.

But as Grant hammered Lee before Richmond, Wing, who had seen his share of the war's suffering, began to lose heart. After Cold Harbor, where 7000 Union soldiers fell in a few hours, Wing decided to resign. At the White House, he gave the President an anguished description of the nightmarish battle. He told how he had wandered through the smoke-filled woods, taking down messages from the dying for wives and children at home.

Lincoln sighed deeply. "And after that you go back to the army—are going back again," he said. "Why, boy, you shame me. You've done your part; anybody would say that. You could quit in honor, but you stick. I wonder if I could do that? I don't believe I would. There's many a night, Henry, that I plan to resign. I wouldn't run again now if I didn't know these other fellows couldn't save the Union on their platforms whatever they say. I can't quit, Henry; I have to stay. But you could, and you don't."

Wing rose, his face flushed, and for the first time the President sensed what was going on in his mind. Softly, tenderly, he asked: "I reckon we won't quit, will we, Henry?"

Henry Wing went back to the army. In fact, his love of newspapering revived, and before the war was over he bought a controlling interest in the Litchfield, Connecticut, *Inquirer*. But he stayed with the Union Army until Robert E. Lee surrendered to Ulysses Grant at Appomattox. With a shrewdness that proved he was a born newspaperman, Wing cooked up a scheme to scoop other reporters on this last and biggest story of the war. Grant and Lee were still in the McLean house, discussing the surrender terms, when a Union staff officer came out on the porch, took off his hat and wiped his forehead with his handkerchief three times. Wing bounded aboard Jess, and headed for the telegraph office at a full gallop. The officer's signal meant that Lee had accepted Grant's surrender terms.

A new kind of America emerged from the war, a nation not merely politically reunited, but bound by far closer psychological ties. The very consciousness of the meaning of the word American had been changed, and not a little of this change could be traced to the Civil War reporters. For the first time in American history, the nation had been united by a continuous, almost simultaneous flow of news. Everyone was linked in a different, more vital way to the nation's leaders. The poet James Russell Lowell never forgot the way he felt when he saw the headlines on April 10, 1865, announcing that the war was over at last. "I felt a strange and tender exultation. I wanted to laugh and I wanted to cry and ended . . . by feeling devoutly thankful. There is something magnificent in a country to love."

5. NEW GIANTS AND NEW FRONTIERS

As surely as newspapers had changed the nation, the war had changed newspapers. Editorials continued to be printed as they are today. But people no longer bought a paper because they happened to agree with the political opinion or philosophy of life held by the men who wrote it. A well-known author wrote in 1866, "The power and success of a newspaper depend wholly and absolutely on its success in getting and its skill in exhibiting the news. . . . The news is the point of rivalry; it is that for which 19/20th of the people buy newspapers. . . ." By 1870, there were 4500 newspapers in the United States—a third of all the papers in the world. Foreign visitors marveled at the "universality of print."

To this news revolution was soon added another battle cry that signaled still another stage in the maturity of the American newspaper. Whitelaw Reid, who succeeded Horace Greeley as the editor of the *Tribune,* sounded it first.

Independent journalism! That is the watchword of the future in the profession. An end of concealments because it would hurt the party; an end of one-sided expositions . . . ; an end of assaults that are not believed fully just but must be made because the exigency of party warfare demands them; an end of slanders that are known to be slanders . . . of doctoring reports of public opinion . . . of half truths . . . that is the end to which to every perplexed conscientious journalist a new and beneficent declaration of independence affords.

New York's newspapers soon had a magnificent opportunity to prove that they meant these words. The city was being governed by a band of crooks under the leadership of William Marcy Tweed, the grand sachem of the Tammany Society. Thanks to a city charter which he wrote himself, Tweed was free to do almost anything. But in July 1871, after three years of uncontrolled plundering, a rival of Tweed, ex-Sheriff James O'Brien, turned over to the New York *Times* transcripts of the City Comptroller's records. Tweed frantically sent one of his henchmen, Richard B. ("Slippery Dick") Connolly to bribe editor George Jones of the *Times,* reportedly offering him $5 million to burn the evidence.

"I don't think the devil will ever make a higher bid for me than that," Jones said.

"Why with that sum you could go to Europe and live like a prince," Connolly said.

"Yes," said Jones, "but I should know that I was a rascal."

On July 8, 1871, the *Times* began its exposé. The paper told how phony leases, padded bills, false vouchers, unnecessary repairs, outrageous kickbacks and raised accounts enabled Tweed and his cronies to steal millions from the city each month. Tweed fought back, instituting a suit to eject the *Times* from its premises. Other New York newspapers rallied to the *Times*'s defense. Thomas Nast, cartoonist for *Harper's Weekly*, the nation's most influential magazine, joined in the attack.

On July 22, the *Times* under a front page headline, "THE SECRET ACCOUNTS: PROOFS OF UNDOUBTED FRAUDS BROUGHT TO LIGHT," fired a real broadside. The figures "copied with scrupulous fidelity from Comptroller Connolly's books" appalled New York and the nation. On one day alone, furniture charges for the new courthouse were listed at $129,469.48. It was soon evident that the Tweed Ring had looted at least $75 million and possibly $200 million from the city treasury.

At the next election, New Yorkers voted Tweed into oblivion and he was indicted on more than a hundred counts. Tweed died in jail, and his followers took refuge abroad.

Around the nation, other papers took fire from the sight of Tweed's downfall. The St. Louis *Democrat* exposed the Whiskey Ring, organized in St. Louis to defraud the federal government of tax revenue. In Kansas City, the *Evening Star*, headed by dynamic William Rockhill Nelson, made "community service" its byword and attacked gambling and vice rings, unpaved streets, shabby buildings, fraudulent elections.

Newspapers were reaching out in other directions as well. The world as well as the nation was becoming their beat. The man who proved this dramatically in 1872 was James Gordon Bennett, Jr., son of the founder of the New

York *Herald.* An eccentric who ran his paper from Paris, Bennett was fond of saying: "I make news." When a Scottish explorer-missionary named David Livingstone landed on the shore of East Africa near the mouth of the Ruvuma River and disappeared into the bush, the world joined in puzzling over his fate. But no one did anything about it. The Royal Geographical Society of England which had sponsored Livingstone's trip did not have enough money to send an expedition to find him.

Bennett summoned to Paris one of the *Herald*'s best reporters, Henry Stanley, an adventurer who had served in both the Confederate and Union armies, and later covered the Indian wars in the northwest United States and a French expedition into Abyssinia in 1868. Bennett gave Stanley $5000 and told him to draw more money in $5000-lump sums whenever he needed it. Price was no object. He only had one command to fulfill: *"Find Livingstone."*

Almost two years later, Stanley finally struck out from Zanzibar into the jungle with two other white men, thirty armed natives and one hundred and fifty pack animals. Fighting fever and hostile natives, they struggled through the swamps of equatorial Africa.

Stanley's dispatches were read with hypnotic fascination around the world. He told of Arab slave traders who threatened him with death, fierce, spear-waving tribesmen who demanded tribute before allowing him to pass across their territory. ("Does the white man mean to go on without paying?") Finally, after nine months in the jungle, he was circling the shores of Lake Tanganyika when he met a native who strode up to him and said: "How do you do, sir."

He was one of Dr. Livingstone's servants and he swiftly led Stanley and his party to a village where an old man awaited him, surrounded by "most respectable Arabs." The natives, seeming to sense the drama in the occasion, sang and beat their drums as Stanley strode toward the emaciated figure.

> Doffing my helmet, I bowed and said in inquiring tone, "Dr. Livingstone, I presume."
> Smiling cordially, he lifted his cap and answered briefly, "Yes."

Experts at first pooh-poohed Stanley's accomplishment. One Britisher declared that Livingstone had discovered Stanley. But when the newspaperman returned to civilization, he read a paper to the Royal Geographical Society of the results of Livingstone's recent explorations and one of his sharpest critics had to admit "the great value of Mr. Stanley's services." Livingstone, broken in health, died a few months later leading an expedition to search for the source of the Nile. Stanley, convinced that Africa was the continent of the future, devoted many of the remaining years of his life to further explorations, notably in the Congo. His stories of pygmies, cannibals, exotic animals, rubber-producing plants and other wonders of the Dark Continent brought on the colonial "scramble for Africa" among the great European powers.

Meanwhile, American newspapermen were busy on another frontier. As wagon trains, gold miners, gamblers and ranchers rode west, printers and reporters went with them. Like their predecessors along an earlier border, they soon learned to combine writing with marksmanship, especially when they tended to lecture their readers on the local need for less gambling and drinking and more respectability. William Newton Byers tried this in a frontier town named Denver. He was marched to a saloon at gunpoint and probably would have been lynched but for the fact that a noted gunfighter of the day, Charlie Harrison, took pity on him and "persuaded the rest of the crowd to let the newspaperman live." Unrepentant, Byers went back and turned his newspaper office into a fortress; every man in the building was armed with a rifle or a shotgun. When his enemies attempted to launch an attack from the building across the street, all-out war erupted and Byers shot one of their advance guard dead. Other editors, not so handy with a gun, chose to "strike out through the sagebrush" when they saw a reader coming with blood in his eye.

Western editors shot at and abused each other with equal abandon. Ned McGowan of the Sacramento *Phoenix* had the following to say about Thomas S. King, editor of the San Francisco *Bulletin,* in 1857.

> The life of Thomas S. King, alias
> Slippery Sam
> From earth's center to the sea
> Nature stinks of thine and thee.

Most famous of the Western papers was the Virginia City, Nevada, *Territorial Enterprise.* Built on the prosperity of the famed silver mine, the Comstock Lode, the *Enterprise* was the paper that gave a young Missourian named Samuel Clemens his first chance to sign "Mark Twain" at the bottom of a piece of copy. Twain had a tough time getting aboard the *Enterprise*. It was already famous for its humor, written by now-forgotten but once-famous funny men such as Don De Quille. Like many Western papers, the *Enterprise* specialized in the hoax. De Quille wrote about the "sad fate of an inventor," the tale of a man who created an apparatus to protect him from the heat of the sun while crossing the desert. It succeeded so well that searchers found him in Death Valley frozen to death. He told another one about a windmill designed to move loads of sand and gravel and got numerous inquiries from professional engineers.

Twain swiftly proved he could bat in this big league by writing a column entitled "Massacre on the Giant Forests Surrounding Dutch Nick's on the Carson River." It was a completely imaginary story about a man who went mad because he sold his sound Nevada silver stocks and bought some phony stock in a useless mine. He then proceeded to murder his wife and children. To Twain's astonishment, the story was accepted as literal truth throughout the territory and Twain became famous overnight. Later he said, "The idea that anybody could ever take my massacre for a genuine occurrence never once suggested itself to me. But I found out then, and never have forgotten since, that we never read the dull explanatory surroundings of marvelously exciting things. . . . We skip all that, and hasten to revel in the blood-curdling particulars and be happy."

Like many other Western newspapermen, Twain one day found himself challenged to a duel. His foe was a reporter on a rival daily who disliked some of the things Twain said about him. Mark was more than a little shaky as he rode out into the desert to confront the wrong end of a pistol. But one of his best friends noticed that the other fellow's knees were knocking even louder. While the rival was conferring with his second, Twain's friend, who was a dead shot, snatched the gun out of Mark's hand and blasted a sage hen out of the sky. By the time Twain's opponent turned his head, there stood Mark with a smoking revolver in his hand, the bird at his feet with its head shot off and his friend complimenting him on his Deadeye Dicksmanship. The fellow forthwith dropped his gun and caught the first stagecoach out of town.

Back East, meanwhile, still another kind of excitement was shaking up the newspaper world. It wore skirts and traveled under the name Nellie Bly. Nellie was not America's first newspaperwoman. Ann Royall had published a highly personal Washington paper named *Paul Pry* from 1831 to 1836. Later, columnists such as "Fanny Fern" and "Jenny June" attracted thousands of women readers to top New York papers such as the *World* and the *Tribune* and the *Ledger*. But they wrote columns of comment and advice. Nellie was the first of her sex to make America conscious of the woman reporter. She did it by operating in a style that made Stanley's search for Livingstone look tame.

A 5-foot 3-inch dynamo with mournful gray eyes, Nellie added new dimensions to the reporter's role. She was an accomplished actress and faked her way into the mental

hospital on New York's Blackwell's Island. Her sensational
stories of conditions there brought on a grand jury investigation. Up in Albany, she went to see a certain Mr.
Phelps and pretended she wanted to kill a pending bill. Mr.
Phelps, better known as the lobby king of Albany, named
his price and Nellie went home to tell the whole world he
was a crook. She visited city prisons and forced the government to appoint matrons to handle women prisoners. She
got herself arrested and told the grisly experience in detail.
She made paper boxes in a factory and reported that from
the viewpoint of protecting her virtue, it was the most
dangerous job a girl could hold.

Once, indignant over reports that mashers were annoying young girls who strolled in Central Park, she allowed
one of the boldest to pick her up. He was a veritable Beau
Brummel, complete with cutaway, pomaded curl over his
forehead, waxed whiskers and a sparkling horseshoe pin
in his tie. Nellie exposed him to the world as a fraud who
played the man-about-uptown one day a week and spent
the other six serving drinks in a downtown saloon.

But Nellie's greatest feat was yet to come. In 1888 she
had gone to Joseph Pulitzer, the mercurial editor of the
New York *World,* and asked him to send her around the
world, betting that she could beat the eighty days it took
Jules Verne's mythical hero Phileas Fogg to make the
circuit. Pulitzer turned her down but the following year
on exactly four days' notice, he changed his mind and
Nellie was off. With two small satchels, two frocks, a
toothbrush, some flannel underwear, a bank book, a plaid
ulster and a twenty-four-hour watch, Nellie sped from
ship to train to burro to jinrikisha to sampan to stage-

coach while the *World* published a daily report of her progress. One of the high points was a stop Nellie made in France to visit the aging Jules Verne himself, living in retirement near Amiens. He told her he frankly did not think she could do better than Phileas. This only galvanized Nellie. Through the Suez Canal and on to Singapore she steamed, then to Hong Kong, surviving a monsoon en route, through China to Japan and across the Pacific where the *World* met her with a special train which rushed her across the country.

By now the whole nation was in a frenzy. Crowds jammed stations at every stop and when the train pulled into Jersey City, bands were playing, cannons boomed salutes and the famous and near famous formed a welcoming committee to greet her. She had covered 24,899 miles in 72 days, 6 hours and 11 minutes. Jules Verne sent a telegram congratulating her, a race horse was named after her and Tin Pan Alley rushed to immortalize her in song. Here is how the *World* told her story.

FATHER TIME OUTDONE!
Even Imagination's Record Pales Before
the Performance of the World's
Globe Circler

It is finished.

Sullen echoes of cannon across the grey waters of the Bay and over the roofs and spires of three cities.

People look at their watches. It is only four o'clock. These cannot be the sunset guns.

Is someone dead?

Only an old era. And the booming yonder at the Battery and Fort Green tolls its passing away. The stage coach days are ended and the new age of lightning travel has begun.

And amid all the tumult, walks the little lady, with just a foot of space between her and that madly joyous mob. She is carrying a little walking stick in one hand and with the other waves her checkered little fore and aft traveling cap, and laughs merrily as her name is hoarsely shouted from innumerable throats. Tense faces stare from the long galleries that bend ominously beneath their awful load of humanity. The tops of passenger coaches lying upon the side tracks are black with men and boys. . . .

But the little girl trips gaily along. The circuit of the globe is behind her. Time is put to blush. . . .

Nellie Bly played a vital role in an epic struggle between two newspaper giants, Joseph Pulitzer and William Randolph Hearst. These flamboyant men dominated the newspaper scene in the 1890s and early 1900s, as Bennett and Greeley had led the newspaper world before the Civil War. Pulitzer arrived first. A thin, wiry immigrant from Hungary, he won his first success as a reporter on a German-language paper in St. Louis. A dynamic worker with brilliant ideas on how to create excitement in a newspaper, he next became owner of the St. Louis *Post-Dispatch*. Soon he was a wealthy man, and in 1883, while he was en route to Europe, he bought a sick newspaper, called the New York *World*. It had a circulation of only 15,000 and was losing $40,000 a year.

Pulitzer calmly announced that he would make the paper profitable by following the formula that had made the *Post-Dispatch* a success—it would "expose all fraud and shams, fight all public evils and abuses." To this approach, Pulitzer added catchy headlines such as SCREAM-ING FOR MERCY, ALL FOR A WOMAN'S LOVE, A BRIDE BUT NOT A WIFE, DEATH RIDES THE BLAST, A PREACHER'S PERFIDY, DUKE MEETS HIS DOOM. Within a year, the *World*'s Sunday circulation had reached a hundred thousand and Pulitzer celebrated by firing a hundred-gun salute in City Hall Park and giving every employee a silk top hat.

But overwork broke Pulitzer's health. He became morbidly sensitive to noise and spent almost all his time in soundproof rooms in his mansion or in the quiet cabin of his yacht at sea. He also became almost entirely blind. But he continued to direct his newspapers from a distance, in spite of his physical deficiencies.

Pulitzer's withdrawal from personal leadership, however, opened the door for William Randolph Hearst. The son of a California millionaire, he worked during his senior year in college as a reporter on Pulitzer's *World*, and learned enough to apply his breezy, crusading formula to a sick paper on the other side of the continent, the San Francisco *Examiner*. After building this paper to the highest circulation in San Francisco, Hearst borrowed $7,500,-000 from his mother and invaded New York. He bought the New York *Journal* and hired away Pulitzer's best people. The two giants were soon locked in a furious circulation war. They used stunts and crusades and sensational headlines. Comics were thrown into the battle, one of the most popular being a grimy urchin dressed in a strange yellow nightgown. He was known as "The Yellow Kid." When Hearst hired away from Pulitzer the artist who had created this character, Pulitzer hired another artist to con-

tinue an imitation of the original in the *World*. Seeing the
yellow splashed all over the Sunday papers of both the
World and the *Journal,* another New York newspaperman,
Irvin Wardman, labeled their approach to news "yellow
journalism," a name which stuck, and soon became synony-
mous with sensationalism.

Searching around for a story that would arouse the
public, Hearst discovered the Cuban insurrection. The Cubans had been fighting Spain in a rather confused and des-
ultory way for several years. The Spaniards permitted
newspapermen to enter the island but insisted on imposing
strict censorship. This aroused the antagonism of American reporters, and they consistently sided with the rebels
in their accounts of the struggle. It was also, of course, a
natural inclination of Americans, with a strong revolutionary tradition in their past. Soon the U. S. Senate
Foreign Relations Committee was holding hearings on "the
Cuban problem," basing most of its information on newspaper stories. It issued a report deploring the war and
severely criticizing the brutal way in which the Spaniards
were attempting to suppress the rebellion. A minority
report went even further, asking the President to "inter-
pose his friendly offices with the Spanish government for
the recognition of the independence of Cuba."

As more newspaper stories of Spanish atrocities came
booming into the country, the whole Senate adopted a
similar resolution by a vote of 64 to 6. As far as William
Randolph Hearst was concerned, this practically gave him
the right to demand that the United States declare war on
Spain, on behalf of Cuba. Story after story appeared in the
Journal emphasizing Spanish cruelty. The Spanish general,

Weyler, was converted into a supervillain. WEYLER THROWS NUNS INTO PRISON, BUTCHER WAGES BRUTAL WARFARE ON HELPLESS WOMEN roared typical Hearst headlines.

Hearst ran story after story about heroic Cuban women fighting beside their men. When the Spaniards arrested one pretty young rebel, Evangelina Cisneros, Hearst performed the incredible feat of sending to Havana a reporter who bribed jailers and rescued her from prison. The *Journal* introduced her to New York at a huge rally in Madison Square Garden, and popular enthusiasm was so intense, President McKinley received her at Convention Hall in Washington, D.C., with a hundred thousand spectators cheering madly.

The Cubans, encouraged by American support, became even more rebellious. Riots swept Havana, and the President ordered the battleship *Maine* to move into the harbor of that port, to make sure that American citizens were not endangered. Meanwhile, the *Journal* was devoting the entire front page to a banner headline: NEXT TO WAR WITH SPAIN.

Actually, behind the scenes, the politicians of the two nations were working to avert a clash. But a few days later, a reckless act in Havana harbor gave William Randolph Hearst the war he wanted.

In shrouded Havana harbor, the battleship *Maine* floated at anchor beneath a moonless starry sky. At ten minutes after nine o'clock, the ship's bugler sent taps floating across the placid water. On shore, Havana swayed and rumbaed to the beat of carnival rhythms. Masked crowds swarmed gaily through the streets. Two American reporters, George Bronson Rea and Sylvester Scovel, sat in a sidewalk café and watched them.

Suddenly, thirty minutes after taps, a new sound erupted from the *Maine*—a gigantic ear-shattering explosion that blew out windows and doors all over Havana and almost knocked reporters Rea and Scovel out of their seats. They ran into the street and saw the harbor sky lit by a fierce white glow. Rockets went shrieking into the darkness beyond it, and there were more explosions, not as big as the first one.

Rea and Scovel raced to the docks, shared a boat with the head of the Havana police and rowed out to the burning exploding ship. Fragments of six-inch shells hissed around them. The *Maine* was a sinking wreck. Ashore, the two reporters raced to telegraph the shocking news to America.

Who sank the stubby little battleship remains a mystery to this day. Americans at the time assumed it was the Spanish. It may well have been a Cuban insurgent, anxious to drag the United States into the war. If so, he succeeded. The eyewitness reports of the tragedy from Rea and Scovel made most Americans feel Spain should be punished. Peace negotiations collapsed, and in a few months the United States and Spain were at war. American newsmen immediately revived the Civil War tradition, and dodged bullets and shells beside the soldiers and sailors.

On May 1, 1898, when Commodore George Dewey steamed into Manila harbor with the United States Asiatic Fleet, standing at the commodore's elbow on the bridge of his flagship *Olympia* was Joseph L. Stickney, a reporter for the New York *Herald*. A graduate of the United States Naval Academy, Stickney was an expert on naval warfare, and he jotted in his notebook, moments after he heard it, Dewey's famous order to his executive officer: "You may fire when ready, Gridley." Two other reporters were with the fleet, Edwin W. Harden of the New York *World* and John T. McCutcheon of the Chicago *Record*. They watched in a delirium of excitement, while Dewey wrecked the antiquated Spanish fleet in six hours of fighting, without losing a man.

The reporters' excitement turned to frustration when they realized there was no way to get this first great story of the war to their papers. The Spanish army was in control of Manila, and Dewey did not have enough marines aboard his ships to drive them out. To make sure the

Spanish got no help, Dewey cut the cable to Hong Kong. For five days, the reporters had to grind their teeth while the commodore wrote his dispatches. A cutter was assigned to carry them to Hong Kong, and the three reporters leaped aboard it. Now came an even more maddening problem. Who was going to send his story first? They finally tossed coins. Stickney won. But Harden was a wily reporter in the no-holds-barred tradition Joseph Pulitzer had created at the *World*. He let Stickney send his long, carefully written story at the standard cable rate of 60 cents a word. When his turn came, Harden gave the operator a sly wink and asked to send a sixty-word bulletin at the urgent rate. This would cost him $9.90 a word, but the operator, knowing nothing about the newspaper business, sent it out even before Commodore Dewey's dispatches.

The next day, the New York *World* and the Chicago *Tribune,* which purchased its syndicated service, turned out tens of thousands of extra copies with giant headlines shouting: DIRECT NEWS FROM DEWEY! NOT ONE AMERICAN KILLED! ONLY SIX AMERICANS IN- JURED! ELEVEN SPANISH SHIPS SUNK. Exultantly, the *World* told its readers how their Washington correspondent had awakened President McKinley to show him the dispatch. The President gave "a sigh of relief." For days a wild assortment of rumors about Dewey had been circulating around the world. At one point the Spanish Foreign Office announced a victory for their side. Other European sources said the Americans had won, but Dewey's fleet was a bloody wreck.

At Tampa, Florida, meanwhile, dozens of other correspondents were fighting what they called "the rocking chair war." Tampa was the place where the Americans were gathering ships, men and supplies for the invasion of Cuba. Weeks passed, with little or no war news to report. Government snafus delayed the preparation of both men and ships. To make news, correspondents slipped across the water to Cuba and joined bands of local insurgents. This was risky business. It they were caught, they could be shot as spies. Stephen Crane, already famous as the author of *The Red Badge of Courage,* a novel about the Civil War, was a born daredevil. He told of one trip where, after much marching, the Cubans he was with decided to take a swim. While they were in the water, firing broke out between their sentries and a Spanish patrol. They scampered out of the water, grabbed their guns and went into action dressed in their cartridge belts and nothing more. Later, Crane and another reporter performed the amazing feat of sneaking through the Spanish lines around Santiago and making sketches of the Spanish fleet, which they delivered to the American navy. "The bay was white in the sun, and the great black-hulled armored cruisers were impressive in a dignity massive yet graceful," Crane wrote. He was not, however, impressed with the Cuban army. He told of "pickets in bunches of three . . . coming in to report to the captain, lazily aswing in a hammock."

But the man who made the most excitement in Tampa was William Randolph Hearst. He arrived with a fleet of ten dispatch boats and a staggering twenty-five reporters. At the head of this news-gathering squadron was James Creelman, a small, dark-haired bearded man who had won fame covering the Japanese conquest of Korea in 1894.

Competing with Hearst for attention were America's first two lady war correspondents, Mrs. Kathleen Blake Watkins and Anna Northend Benjamin. They ran into a wall of masculine prejudice, but were undaunted. Mrs. Watkins grimly announced, "I'm going through to Cuba and not all the old generals in the old army are going to stop me." She soon won the respect of skeptical male reporters with her energy and talent. "In a little while she was introducing us to generals and colonels," one reporter admitted. While many newsmen dozed in their rocking chairs or retired to the bar to escape the Tampa heat, Mrs. Watkins trudged through the army camps, and wrote stories full of fascinating local color. In one Western regiment she found six outlaws who had enlisted because they figured the Spaniards could not shoot as straight as a sheriff's posse. Ruefully, a Chicago reporter conceded, "By gosh, for a five-card draw she's hot stuff—steam comes out of her boots all the time and the whole Chicago fire brigade couldn't put her out."

Finally came the day of the invasion. The reporters were not permitted by the army to go in with the first wave of troops. But they were soon ashore, and some of them began mixing fighting and reporting. Handsome Richard Harding Davis, already famous as a war correspondent, teamed up with Theodore Roosevelt, colonel of the regiment he had raised, called the Rough Riders. Studying the country ahead through his field glasses, Davis spotted a Spanish position on a forested mountain. He pointed it out to Roosevelt, and soon the Rough Riders' advance scouts were skirmishing with the Spanish pickets. Davis became so enthused with his impromptu role as a military adviser, he next helped a lieutenant lead a charge against a tin shack defended by the Spanish rear guard. In a letter to his brother, Davis told how he "fired about 20 rounds," and then helped Roosevelt form "a strategy board" before going down the trail "to scout." Historians frequently point out that Theodore Roosevelt's exploits in the Spanish-American War helped make him a presidential candidate. But seldom does anyone mention that it was Richard Harding Davis who wrote most of the Roosevelt-glorifying dispatches. In the charge up San Juan Hill, Davis was only a few steps behind the colonel of the Rough Riders.

Stephen Crane, ever the realist, wired home a drastically different impression of the Rough Riders. "I want to say here plainly that the behavior of these Rough Riders while marching through the woods shook me with terror as I have never before been shaken. . . . This regiment of volunteers knew nothing but their own superb courage. They wound along this narrow path babbling joyously, arguing, recounting and laughing; making more noise than a train going through a tunnel. Anyone could tell . . . we were liable to strike the enemy's outpost but the clatter of tongues did not then cease."

Although he never won as much attention from the public as Creelman or Davis, Crane's war reporting was superb. Like the novelist that he was, he made many of his stories read like fiction. At Guantánamo Bay, he told an unforgettable story of a young marine who stood erect counting the flag signals from the fleet, while bullets splashed the sand around him. Crane did not, of course, bother to mention that he sat at the feet of the signalman, risking the same bullets, watching his lips move as he counted.

But the correspondent who combined reporting and fighting in the most dramatic fashion was James Creelman. Knowing that the Americans planned to attack the key Spanish fortress of El Caney, Creelman struggled through thorn thickets and swamps to a small hill nearby. There, he watched for hours while the Americans crept nearer and nearer to the fort, taking heavy casualties from the deadly Spanish fire. Finally, Creelman moved to the next hill, where he found the general in command of the operation. Bullets were flying all around them—one knocked a button off the general's coat—while Creelman hastily explained that he had found a way to capture the fort. He had spotted a back road up which troops could approach close enough for a bayonet charge. Carried away "by patriotism and excitement," as he told it, Creelman offered to lead the way personally. Here is how he tells the rest of the story:

> We pushed our way through a line of low bushes and started up the hill to the fort. The only weapon I had was a revolver, and the holster was hung around to the back so that I should not be tempted to draw.
>
> When I found myself out on the clear escarped slope in front of the fort and its deadly trench, walking at the head of a storming party, I began to realize that I had ceased to be a journalist and was now—foolishly or wisely, recklessly, mettlesomely or patriotically—a part of the army, a soldier without warrant to kill.
>
> It is only 300 feet to the top of the hill, and yet the slope looked a mile long. . . . There was a barbed wire

fence in front of the trench, a barrier to prevent charges. But it had never occurred to the minds of the Spanish engineers that the accursed Yankees—unsoldierly shopkeepers!—would think of carrying wire nippers in their pockets.

When I reached this fence I was within ten feet of the trench and could see dead hands and faces and the hats of the living soldiers crouching there. A scissors-like motion of the fingers indicated to Captain Haskell that men with wire nippers were needed. Two soldiers ran up and began to sever the wires. . . .

It took but a few seconds to cut a hole in the fence and reach the edge of the trench. It was crowded with dead and dying men. Those who were unhurt were crouching down waiting for the end. . . . A silent signal, and one of the men who had cut the wire fence advanced, and covered the men in the trench with his rifle. A spoken word, and the cowering Spaniards leaped up and raised their hands in a token of surrender. . . . In less time then it takes to write it, the trench was crossed and the open door at the end of the fort was reached.

The scene inside was too horrible for description. Our fire had killed most of the garrison, and the dead and wounded lay on the floor in every conceivable attitude. . . . Just inside the door stood a young Spanish officer, surrounded by his men. . . . Beside him was a soldier holding a ramrod, to which was fastened a white handkerchief . . . a mute appeal for life. . . . I looked about the roofless walls for the flag. It was gone. . . . "A shell carried the flag away," said the Spanish officer. "It is lying outside." Dashing though the door and running around to the side facing El Caney I saw the red and yellow flag lying in the dust, a fragment of the staff still attached to it. I picked it up and wagged it at the entrenched village.

That last bit of display was a mistake. A Spanish sharpshooter smashed Creelman's left arm with a bullet as he waved the flag. Friendly soldiers carried him back down the hill where he tried to write his story. But the wound and the exhausting day-long effort under fire had weakened him badly. He could not get the words down on paper. Suddenly through the haze of heat, like an apparition from another world, came his publisher, William Randolph Hearst, wearing a straw hat with a bright ribbon on his head and a revolver at his belt. Snipers' bullets whined overhead, but the excited Hearst knelt beside his star reporter and took down his dictation of his daredevil exploits. "I'm sorry you're hurt," Hearst crowed, "but wasn't it a splendid fight? We must beat every paper in the world."

Two days later came the climax of the war. AP correspondent George Graham was on the bridge of the USS *Brooklyn*, patrolling off Santiago when he heard a lookout roar: "The enemy ships are coming out."

"Come on, my boy," thundered Commodore Winfield S. Schley, "we'll give it to them now."

The Spanish fleet did not really want to fight—they were only trying to escape the disgrace of capture. Five hours later they were all on the ocean bottom, in one of the wildest, most unorthodox naval battles in history. Hearst dispatch boats darted in and out among the fighting ships. One rescued a Spanish officer and eight sailors. The commander of one dispatch boat, John P. Dunning, leaped aboard the USS *Gloucester* and wangled an interview with the Spanish admiral, Pasqual Cervera, while the defeated commander was still sopping wet. Hearst sprang from another dispatch boat to capture a group of Spanish sailors on a nearby beach at pistol point. George Graham, meanwhile, recorded the battle from the bridge of the USS *Brooklyn.*

Some critics looking back on the war wondered if the correspondents had not turned it into a circus. There is no doubt that it was the last of the romantic wars. But Richard Harding Davis, always generous with praise to his fellow reporters, was also right when he wrote: "The reckless bravery and the unselfishness of the correspondents in the field in Cuba today are beyond parallel."

7. TO THE WESTERN FRONT

It was the golden age of the reporter, and the most golden of them was that handsome daredevil named Richard Harding Davis. Like Nellie Bly, Davis seized the imagination of the country with hair-raising tales of personal adventure. His specialty was not stunts but wars. By the turn of the century, it was a cliché that no war could be a success until Davis had arrived to cover it.

But Davis was more than an adventure storyteller. He was simultaneously a romantic ideal. Charles Dana Gibson used his ruggedly masculine profile for the perfect companion to his "Gibson girls," the glamor figures of the era. Most of all, Davis inspired the young. Author Booth Tarkington recalled years later: "All ages read him, but the young men and young women . . . turned to him when his fame made him their idol. They got many things from him, but above all they lived with a happier bravery because of him."

Davis wrote best-selling novels and hit plays as well as newspaper stories. But it was always the figure of the daring reporter, dodging bullets and outwitting generals that his readers worshiped. From Cuba he dashed to Greece to lie for thirteen hours in a trench while Turkish shells and bullets tore the earth around him. That war was barely over when he was in South Africa to tell the world about British blundering against the Boers. From there, he galloped off to cover Russians and Japanese brawling in Siberia. By now Davis not only wrote news, he was news. When he dashed to Vera Cruz in 1914 for what looked like a war between the United States and Mexico, he boldly led two other correspondents beyond the American lines around the city and only the fact that he was Richard Harding Davis stopped the Mexicans from shooting him as a spy. But all this was mere rehearsal for the big war, in which Richard Harding Davis was to play a historic role.

World War I exploded on an America bewildered by the claims and counterclaims of the great powers. Were it not for American reporters, the nation might have remained at the mercy of this propaganda barrage, until it decided both sides were wrong and retreated into cynical indifference. Although both the French and British armies refused to accredit correspondents, this did not stop American reporters with their see-it-for-myself tradition. One of the first to go into action was Richard Harding Davis. In the summer of 1914, the German army began rolling through Belgium. The Kaiser's political spokesmen denounced this tiny country's neutrality as a "scrap of paper." Davis rushed to Brussels and then with typical audacity followed the German advance, determined to reach the front lines. Instead, he was arrested and came within a whisker of being executed as a spy. After almost two days of bullying interrogation the Germans let him go, with orders to cover fifty miles back to Brussels in forty-eight hours or be shot on sight.

In spite of the fact that one of his shoes wore out and his foot turned into a piece of raw hamburger, Davis made it back to the Belgian capital inside this murderous deadline. Smuggling out his dispatches with the help of a resourceful young Englishman, he awoke the world to the German menace—and simultaneously wrote what is considered one of the great war stories of all time.

. . . For seven hours the (German) army passed in such solid columns that not once might a taxicab or trolley pass through the city. Like a river of steel it flowed, grey and ghostlike. Then as dusk came and as thousands of horses hoofs and thousands of iron boots continued to tramp forward, they struck tiny sparks from the stones, but the horses and the men who beat out the sparks were invisible.

At midnight pack wagons and siege guns were still passing. At 7 this morning I was awakened by the tramp of men and bands playing jauntily. Whether they marched all night or not I do not know; but now for 26 hours the grey army has rumbled by with the mystery of fog and the pertinacity of a steamroller. . . .

To perfect this monstrous engine with its pontoon bridges, its wireless, its hospitals, its airplanes that in rigid alignment sail before it, its field telephones that as it advanced strung wires over which for miles the vanguard talked to the rear, all modern inventions had been prostituted. To feed it, millions of men had been called from homes, offices and workshops; to guide it, for years the minds of the high born, with whom it is a religion and a disease, had been solely concerned.

It is perhaps the most efficient organization of modern

times; and its purpose only is death. Those who cast it loose upon Europe are military mad. And they are only a very small part of the German people. But to preserve their class they have in their own image created this terrible engine of destruction. For the present it is their servant, but "though the mills of God grind slowly, yet they grind exceeding small." And, like Frankenstein's monster, this monster to which they gave life, may turn and rend them.

The Germans decided to get Davis out of Belgium as fast as possible. They threw him aboard a train packed with captured French and British soldiers. By accident, they railroaded him into one of the biggest stories of the war. On the 27th of August the train pulled into the university city of Louvain. The whole world seemed to be on fire. The Germans were destroying everything, even the ancient university and library, because snipers had killed a few of their soldiers. The moment he was freed (thanks to the efforts of American diplomats), Davis rushed to London and told the world what he thought of German barbarity.

Outside the station in the public square the people of Louvain passed me in an unending procession, women bare headed, weeping, men carrying the children asleep on their shoulders, all hemmed in by the shadowy army of grey wolves. Once they were halted and among them were marched a line of men. They well knew their fellow townsmen. These were on their way to be shot. . . . You felt it was only a nightmare, cruel and uncivilized. And then you remember the German Emperor has told us what it is. It is his Holy War.

Back in America, Davis launched an all-out campaign to rally his native land against the Prussian menace. He wrote articles, gave lectures, urging America to build up its sadly depleted army and navy. He even joined a summer training camp for volunteers and trudged miles under a scorching sun, ignoring pains about his heart and several fainting spells. Then he returned to Europe and covered the ill-fated British campaign in the Mediterranean. Doctors ordered him home to rest, but he insisted on throwing himself once more into the fight for preparedness. He was writing an article on this all-important subject when he was struck down by a heart attack. He was only fifty-two.

Meanwhile, other American reporters had rushed to France, and a stunned, horrified America was soon reading about the carnage on the Western Front. Men were being slaughtered on a scale never before seen in the history of warfare. But it was not so easy to describe the front-line fighting as it had been in the Civil War and the Spanish-American War. Both the German and the Allied governments insisted on censoring all news. The reporters were forced to rely on descriptions of soldiers and ambulance drivers who had been at the front. These were often vivid enough. Wythe Williams of the New York *Times* electrified readers with his vivid story of how Paris taxicabs rushed the last French reinforcements to the Marne in time to stop the German advance within a day's march of the capital. But Williams was so frustrated by the omnipotent censorship that he soon gave up reporting and drove an ambulance himself for several months. Finally, when the war had relapsed into a stalemate, he did receive permission to visit the front lines.

In the second year of the war, another American reporter was a witness—and became a victim—of imperial Germany's ruthless indifference to international law. Will Irwin was just behind the front lines, watching a French division in action, when he suddenly saw "a cloud of vapor, greenish grey and iridescent" rolling toward the Allied trenches. It was poison gas. Irwin bitterly noted that in 1907 Germany had signed the Hague Convention, in which the great powers agreed to outlaw such a weapon. "The Germans who charged in behind the vapor met no resistance at all, the French at their front being virtually paralyzed," Irwin wrote.

Caught up in the retreat, Irwin found himself surrounded by coughing, bleeding men, and he did his best to help them. Suddenly he found himself coughing violently. "The air seemed to burn," he wrote. He was lucky. He had only got a mild dose of the gas. He recovered, but not before he spent a lot of time "haunting the hospitals. . . ."

News in this world war was not confined to the battlefronts in Europe. Wilbur Forrest of the United Press was in his office in London in mid-1915 when he heard that the British liner *Lusitania* had been torpedoed off the Irish coast. Forrest rushed by train and boat to Queenstown, Ireland, where he talked to dozens of survivors. He sent out 7000 words of cabled copy, describing to a shocked world how the ship had been sunk without warning, drowning 1153 persons, including 114 Americans.

Next onto the center of the newspaper stage sprang a

twenty-nine-year-old Chicagoan named Floyd Gibbons. He was already famous for his daring and flamboyance. In 1916, the Mexican bandit Pancho Villa shot up several towns along the Rio Grande border and the United States sent an expeditionary force in pursuit of him. Villa boasted that he would kill any gringo on sight. Gibbons laughed at his threats and strolled into the hills alone, allowed himself to be captured by Villa's men and talked the bandit into a sensational interview. Now Gibbons was on his way to cover the war in Europe. He decided that the best way to begin his career as a war correspondent would be to get torpedoed. He made a special study of ships going to Europe, and finally chose the British Cunard Line steamer, *Laconia.*

At 10:30 P.M. on February 25, 1917, Gibbons was in his stateroom aboard the *Laconia* when he heard "a muffled noise like the slamming of some large door at a good distance away." It was the torpedo he had predicted the *Laconia* was sure to meet. With admirable foresight, he had brought along a special life preserver, a large bottle of fresh water, electric flashlights and a flask of brandy. These helped him survive, and soon Americans were reading Gibbons' vivid, firsthand story of how it felt to be torpedoed in the middle of the Atlantic. He even managed to exchange a few words—it was not really an interview— with the captain of the submarine.

A few months later, America, infuriated by German insults on the high seas, declared war. No less than 411 American reporters followed the American army to France. Imitating the Allied governments, the American army insisted on imposing a rigid censorship. But American reporters were not much different in character and temperament from the Bohemians who had riled generals in the Civil War. The censors were soon getting gray hairs trying to keep them in line.

It was absolutely forbidden, the army informed the gentlemen of the press, to mention the port at which AEF Commander in Chief John J. Pershing landed in England. Floyd Gibbons promptly filed the following cable:

> Pershing landed at British port today and was greeted by the Lord Mayor of Liverpool.

The censor, obviously not the brightest man in the army, let this go out. He was infuriated by the inevitable horselaugh he got when it was published in America. The censor decided to get even. When the first American artillery battery went into action, a group of correspondents was invited to witness the event. The censor carefully omitted Gibbons' name from the list. On the great day, the reporters waited patiently behind the lines for the artillerymen to appear. After a frustrating delay, they finally rolled past, en route to the front. From one of the last caissons a very familiar character grinned and waved jauntily to his fellow newsmen. "Hey," Damon Runyon yelled, "there's Gibbons. How the hell did he get there?" While the censor fumed, Gibbons joined the group, watched the artillerymen fire the first shell and then serenely accepted it from his friends in the battery as a personal souvenir. Only when the agitated censor explained that he was ordered to send the shell case to President Wilson did Gibbons reluctantly surrender it.

On June 6, 1918, the U. S. Marines went into action against crack German units entrenched in Belleau Wood. Beside them, risking the same storm of machine-gun bullets, dashed Floyd Gibbons. This time his luck ran out. He went down with three bullets in his body. One tore out his eye. Gibbons went on to cover a dozen more wars, wearing an eye patch that became his trademark.

Not all reporters concentrated on the brutal business in the front lines. Heywood Broun wrote a revealing, thoughtful profile of General John J. Pershing. He followed the general around for three weeks, wryly noting that he was never on time for appointments, that he spoke very bad French and was an absolute fanatic about details. "He can read a man's soul through his boots or his buttons," Broun wrote. He quoted a younger officer as saying Pershing's favorite military leader was Joshua "because he made the sun and moon stand at attention." Yet he admired the way Pershing concerned himself with every conceivable aspect of the war. He watched him discussing onions with cooks, he climbed with him into hayloft billets where the men slept, held his nose while peering down sewage systems. He made it clear that Pershing was not popular with his men. "No one will ever call him Papa Pershing," Broun wrote. But he also noted that Marshal Joseph Joffre, the French commander who had won this nickname, was not a very good general. Some members of Pershing's staff thought Broun ought to be arrested, and possibly shot, for speaking so disrespectfully of the general. But Pershing never showed the slightest resentment toward Broun for what he wrote, perhaps because he knew it was true.

Even more unusual than Broun was a reporter who

worked for the army newspaper, *The Stars and Stripes*.
His name was Alexander Woollcott and he was the kind of
soldier that would have driven General Pershing insane, if
he ever got a look at him. A fellow reporter described his
uniform as "soiled, sagging and corrugated with unex-
pected bulges." In the front lines, Woollcott carried a fry-
ing pan strapped around his waist, and when the weather
grew chilly, he wore an old gray shawl across his shoulders.
He regarded the war as little more than an annoying in-
trusion on his main interest, the world of the theater and
literature. One day, he was violently offended when a
fellow correspondent criticized one of his favorite ac-
tresses, Maude Adams. Before Woollcott could reply, the
Germans fired a barrage, and both men dived into a muddy
shell hole. While the shrapnel whined overhead, Woollcott
looked up and said, "I have never heard anything so
preposterous. To me Maude Adams as Peter Pan was gay
and spirited and altogether as charming as the silver star on
top of the tree on Christmas morning." Yet Woollcott was
a genius at describing the human side of the war. He told
stories about doughboys and their adopted French dogs,
described life in the hospitals and on the long, dreary
marches between battles.

For most reporters, outwitting the censor remained the
big problem. It was hard for them to understand that the
French, particularly, saw the war as a fight for self-preserva-
tion, and simply would not tolerate anyone who broke the
rules. In all-out war, news was a weapon which played
a potent role in maintaining morale on the homefront.
Wythe Williams mailed an article back to America, describing why an Allied offensive had been a disastrous fail-

ure. His credentials were immediately suspended, and he was ordered out of France. But Georges Clemenceau, the new premier of France, had been a newspaperman, and he revoked the order.

Fred Ferguson of the United Press was one of the few reporters who figured out a way to beat the censors. He heard through a friend at American headquarters that there would soon be an offensive launched by the AEF at St. Mihiel. He wrote a series of bulletins with the time left blank describing each objective, and reporting that the Americans had captured it. He turned these over to the field censor, and asked him to send them out the moment he got good news from the front. Then, for a final bit of byplay, he took his two hottest competitors out for a long ride in a hired car on the day that the offensive was launched. The Germans were retreating even before the Americans attacked at St. Mihiel, and the doughboys reached their objectives quickly. Ferguson's prearranged bulletins went out even faster than he hoped. By the time he and his competitors got back to headquarters, there were congratulatory telegrams for Ferguson from his boss and angry "rockets" for the other correspondents, demanding to know why they weren't on the job.

One of the "rocketed" reporters, Hank Wales of the International News Service, soon topped Ferguson with a different kind of scoop. Combining good luck and some fast talking, he became the only reporter to witness the execution of the Dutch dancer Gertrude Margarete Zelle, better known as Mata Hari. Wales packed all the pathos and tension of the pretty, dark-haired spy's final hours into his description. He told how Mata Hari, convinced that she would be reprieved at the last moment, refused a blindfold and faced her executioners serenely, almost confidently. The firing squad raised their guns and pulled the triggers.

She did not die as actors and moving picture stars would have us believe the people die when they are shot. She did not throw up her hands nor did she plunge straight forward or straight back. Instead she seemed to collapse, slowly, inertly she settled to her knees, her head up always and without the slightest change of expression on her face. For the fraction of a second it seemed she tottered there on her knees gazing directly at those who had taken her life. Then she fell backward, bending at the waist with her legs doubled up beneath her. She lay prone, motionless, with her face turned toward the sky.

In the fall of 1918, as Allied offensives rolled forward all along the Western Front, it became obvious to the reporters that the one big story still left to tell was the news that the war was over. They all knew that it had to be news, not rumor. On September 16, 1918, the New York *Times* wrote an editorial calling on the Allies to accept some vague peace feelers from Germany's war partner, Austria-Hungary. The *Times* was attacked and criticized by everyone from President Wilson to the man in the street for being pro-German. The closer the Allies got to victory, the more tension between the competing journalists built up. The Germans, desperately hoping to avoid unconditional surrender, decided to take advantage of it. One of their secret agents bribed someone in Allied headquarters in Paris to send a phony telegram signed by the

American naval attaché, to the navy officers in Brest, announcing that the war was over. Roy Howard, the president of the United Press, happened to be in the French port, on his way home the day the telegram arrived— November 7, 1918. Admiral Henry B. Wilson, in command of U.S. forces in French waters, showed him the telegram and said: "The armistice has been signed."

"Is it official?" Howard asked.

"Official, hell. I should say it is official. I just received this over my direct wire from the embassy. It's the official announcement."

The admiral had sent the telegram to the local Brest newspaper. French men and women were celebrating in the streets outside his office. Their cheers convinced Howard, and he flashed a bulletin to New York:

UNIPRESS NEWYORK—URGENT. ARMISTICE ALLIES GERMANY SIGNED ELEVEN SMORNING. HOSTILITIES CEASED TWO SAFTEROON. SEDAN TAKEN SMORNING BY AMERICANS.

The UP promptly released the story throughout the United States.

PARIS, NOVEMBER 7 (UP)—THE WAR IS OVER. GERMANY AND THE ALLIES SIGNED AN ARMISTICE AT 11 A.M. TODAY, HOSTILITIES CEASING THREE HOURS LATER. AS MARSHAL FOCH'S TERMS ARE KNOWN TO INCLUDE PROVISIONS WHICH WILL PREVENT RESUMPTION OF HOSTILITIES, THE GREATEST WAR OF ALL TIME HAS COME TO AN END.

Berserk celebrations swept American cities and towns. People danced in the streets. Strangers shook hands and embraced each other. At two o'clock the same day, the joy turned sour when the United States Government in Washington issued a formal announcement that the Germans had not signed armistice terms. Around the same time, in Brest, an appalled Roy Howard was told by an equally disturbed Admiral Wilson that he had just received another telegram from the American embassy in Paris, announcing that the armistice message was "unconfirmable." The desperate Howard filed a correction, but it was too late to prevent the "phony armistice." The following day, when Germany requested armistice talks, they were in a much better bargaining position. The Allied governments, having seen firsthand how deeply their peoples wanted peace, were in no position to refuse to meet the Germans. It was one more proof of the enormous importance of news in the modern world.

Meanwhile, in the far West another kind of newspaper
drama was reaching a climax. It was in some ways the
biography of a single man—Fremont Older. Born in a
Wisconsin log cabin in 1856, Older worked his way across
the nation as a tramp printer and reporter, tasting some
of the wilder varieties of Western journalism until he arrived in San Francisco in 1895, where he soon became
managing editor of the *Bulletin*. It was an era when
California was in the grip of almost unbelievable political
corruption, and Older, tall, strong-jawed with a frontier
marshal's mustache, decided to fight it.

Older aimed his biggest guns at the San Francisco political machine which was bossed by one Abe Ruef. The
editor's sensational exposés brought a team of federal
investigators to San Francisco. Hounded by still more
revelations, Ruef collapsed and confessed that he had dis-
tributed millions in graft, payoffs from restaurants, brothel
owners, industrialists buying favors. Infuriated, Older's
enemies tried to dynamite his home and once actually

kidnaped him. He escaped with his life only because the gunman assigned to take care of him lost his nerve.

During the trial of Ruef and his chief cohort, Mayor Eugene Schmitts, a gunman strode into the courtroom and fired a bullet into the head of Prosecutor Francis J. Heney. But Ruef and Schmitts were convicted and a brilliant young lawyer, Hiram W. Johnson, who replaced the wounded Heney, became governor of California and opened a new era in the politics of the Golden State.

Older took on an even bigger battle in 1916. A home-made bomb exploded on the corner of Steuart and Market streets as a Preparedness Day parade was streaming past. Fifty persons were killed or maimed. The authorities promptly arrested a labor agitator named Tom Mooney and his henchman, Warren Billings. A hothead, noted for his appeals to violence, Mooney was convicted largely on the testimony of a single man, Frank Oxman—"The honest cattleman from Oregon"—who swore that he saw Mooney lean from a car and plant the suitcase loaded with explosives against a brick wall. While Mooney was in jail awaiting sentence, a labor leader brought Older a copy of a letter Oxman had written to a friend in Illinois, inviting him to come West and join him in perjury.

Older despised Mooney as a threat to the peace of the nation. He later said that he was convinced that Mooney should have been in jail for a dozen other crimes, but his newspaperman's credo could not permit any man to be railroaded into the death chamber. A few weeks before Mooney was to be sentenced, the *Bulletin* exploded in giant headlines proclaiming a frame-up. Oxman's letters were published and Older sent his crack reporters swarm-

ing up and down the state to dig out further evidence that a
reckless district attorney had committed a terrible injustice.

Older was denounced as a Communist. Old friends cut
him on the street; he became the loneliest man in San
Francisco. Finally, even his publisher turned against him
and ordered him to suspend the investigation or resign.
By now a concerned President Wilson had persuaded California's governor to grant Mooney a stay of execution.
Another federal investigating team descended upon San
Francisco. Older told his publisher to go to hell and moved
over to become managing editor of the rival *Call*. (Without him, in a few years the *Bulletin* dwindled into financial
collapse and Older had the grim satisfaction of buying and
merging it with the *Call*.) He added his reporters to the
federal task force that was studying the Mooney case.
It was an Older man who dug up witnesses who proved
that the Honest Cattleman was not even in San Francisco
when the bomb exploded.

One night the government investigators secretly
brought to Older the shocking record of their findings.
It revealed the district attorney as a blatant jury rigger and
witness buyer who also spent an astonishing amount of his
private and official hours with ladies of questionable reputation. There was also vivid evidence of fixing in other
cases, including the bribing of a judge of the state supreme
court. Older took this "Densmore report," as it was to be
called, and printed it in full. It ran nine full pages in the
Call and blew the district attorney out of office, exposed
the Supreme Court justice and saved Tom Mooney's life.

But the prejudice toward Mooney was so strong, the
officials did not dare to set him free. His sentence was

commuted to life imprisonment. For the next eighteen years Older continued to crusade for Mooney. Witness after witness, official after official, admitted their part in creating the rigged trial. Even the judge who had sentenced him said he deserved a new trial. But Mooney never got it, and Fremont Older died in 1935, his last crusade unfulfilled. But four years later a new governor, elected on a campaign pledge to free Tom Mooney, kept his promise and what has been called the American Dreyfus case ended in another newspaper victory.

While Older was fighting his lonely battle for Mooney, two young reporters in Chicago solved a murder which quickly became a symbol of a problem we still discuss— "the younger generation." Reporters were used to murders in crime-ridden Chicago in the 1920s. But the senseless slaying of Bobby Franks, the fourteen-year-old son of a wealthy South-side watch manufacturer, after he had been kidnaped and his family asked for $10,000 ransom, seemed more of a puzzle than anything else.

When the Chicago *Daily News* broke the story on May 22, 1924, two cub reporters on the *News,* James W. Mulroy and Alvin H. Goldstein, took a special interest in it. The murdered boy had been kidnaped on a street near Goldstein's home. Discussing the story in a University of Chicago fraternity house, Goldstein struck up a conversation with Richard Loeb, eighteen, who, a year earlier, was the youngest man ever to be graduated from the University of Michigan. Loeb offered to drive the two reporters around town in his car. He even gave them advice on how to solve one of the key riddles in the mystery. Mr. Franks had been summoned to a drugstore

by a phone call moments before he had been told his
boy's body had been found. The shock erased the address
of the drugstore from the father's mind. He could only
remember that it had been on East 63rd Street. "The
way I figure it," Loeb told the reporters, "the kidnappers
wouldn't have been waiting for him in the store. For all
they knew, he might have tipped off the cops. Bet you
they were going to telephone him there with instructions.
Let's see if we can find a place where they got phone calls
asking for Franks."

The trio canvassed drugstores on 63rd Street until they
found a porter who had received two phone calls for Mr.
Franks on the previous day. Suddenly one of the reporters
remembered a remark that Loeb had made while they were
driving around town. "If I was going to kill any kid I'd
pick on just such a fresh little ———— as that Franks kid."
Meanwhile, police had found a pair of horn-rimmed glasses
near Bobby's body. They were traced to Richard Loeb's
closest friend, Nathan F. Leopold, Jr., nineteen, Phi Beta
Kappa graduate of the University of Chicago and a stu-
dent at the university's law school.

Arrested on the testimony of the Leopold family chauffeur, who said he saw the youths washing the interior of
a rented auto, the two steadfastly denied their guilt. How
could they break them down? The police were baffled, but
reporters Goldstein and Mulroy were still at work. Out to
the University of Chicago campus they dashed and in fac-
ulty files found samples of typewriting done by Leopold
on the very typewriter that produced the kidnapers' ran-
som letter. The arrogant young men, who thought they
had committed the perfect crime (they had thrown Leo-

pold's typewriter into a lagoon), wavered when they were confronted with this evidence. The two cub reporters now delivered the knockout punch. They rounded up four college witnesses who appeared at police headquarters at midnight to shatter the last alibis—and the nerve—of the two kidnapers.

Appalled by their candid admission that they had kidnaped and killed Franks largely for kicks, the nation began to wonder for the first time where its youth was heading. Only a masterful defense by the famed attorney Clarence Darrow saved the two thrill killers from a death sentence. Meanwhile, the *Daily News* was able to boast that its two cubs had "contributed more than most of the police force and legions of rival newsmen combined" to the solution of the mystery. It was, they said, the "realization of the dreams of all the thousands of cubs who come stumbling into the dusty local rooms of all the newspapers of the land, green and unskilled and ambitious. To jump from picture chasing to triumph over the whole town in the biggest story of a generation."

Reporting sensational revelations about the great and famous, giving eyewitness accounts of world history in the process of changing or solving crimes—these had by now become basic newspaper achievements. But could a newspaper make its readers care about a tragedy in the life of an obscure, unknown average man? A reporter named "Skeets" Miller of the Louisville *Courier Journal* risked his life to add this new dimension to the power of the printed word. The story began when a young man named Floyd Collins, fond of exploring the underground caverns

of his native Kentucky, was trapped by a cave-in about
one hundred feet below the surface. When Miller arrived
on the scene, he found Collins' friends sitting around idly
wondering how soon Collins would extricate himself. Reporter Miller decided to see for himself. Here is the story of
his journey.

> I was lowered by my heels into the entrance of Sand
> Cave. The passageway is about five feet in diameter. After
> reaching the end of an 80 foot drop I reached fairly level
> ground for a moment.
>
> From there I had to squirm like a snake. Water covers
> almost every inch of the ground and after the first few
> feet I was wet through and through. Every moment it got
> colder. It seemed that I would crawl forever, but after
> going about 90 feet I reached a very small compartment,
> slightly larger than the remainder of the channel.
>
> This afforded a breathing spell before I started again on
> toward the prisoner. The dirty water splashed in my face
> and numbed my body, but I couldn't stop.
>
> Finally I slid down an 8 foot drop and a moment
> later saw Collins and called to him. He mumbled an answer.
> My flashlight revealed . . . the purple of his lips, the
> pallor on his face and I realized that something must be
> done before long if this man is to live. . . .

Miller's dispatches from the scene created a national
sensation. Day after day millions of Americans, who would
not ordinarily have given more than a passing thought to
Collins' dilemma, read about him on page one. Five more
times, Miller crept down that slimy tunnel to interview
the trapped man and chip away at the rock and earth that

trapped him. It was a hopeless fight from the start. Miller described the torturous progress.

Thirteen other men crawl in behind me and pass a small chip hammer along to me. With this I work as best I can enlarging the cave and as soon as I have succeeded in getting loose a large piece, I pass it back to the men behind me and in this way it is relayed out to the entrance.

It is terrible inside. The cold, dirty water numbs us as soon as we start in. We have come to dread it, but each of us tells ourselves that our suffering is as nothing compared to Collins'.

In desperation, expert miners began sinking a shaft from above, even though their drilling created the possibility of another collapse which would bury Collins for good. "In millions of American homes," wrote one reporter, "the suspense became personal, the sound of the miners boring was an audible throb." On the eighteenth day of the ordeal, disaster piled upon tragedy. An underground upheaval threw the floor of the cave upward, cutting Collins off from his rescuers. Miller sent a last dispatch to his paper.

In death, as in the last week or more of his life, Floyd Collins must remain entrapped in Sand Cave. . . . The tomb is sealing itself in collapse. . . . Soon Floyd Collins will be lost forever in a cave he died to explore.

As the twenties faded into the thirties, more and more newspapers joined the war on organized crime. The glaring searchlight of publicity on Chicago's baron, Al Capone, played a key role in putting him behind bars for income tax evasion. But the man who hypnotized the country as a symbol of reckless violence was John Dillinger, the Indiana bad boy who declared war on the banks of the United States. Then Dillinger made the mistake of shooting down an agent of the Federal Bureau of Investigation. The G-men stalked him relentlessly. Finally they traced him to Chicago. As the net tightened, a reporter in New York City, Jack Lait, got a phone call from the son of a Chicago policeman for whom he had once done a favor. "I'd spent the flower of my youth in the windy burg," Lait wrote later. "I addressed at least 10,000 cops by their first names." Without asking questions, Lait dashed to Chicago and proceeded to beat the entire newspaper fraternity to the crime story of the decade.

John Dillinger, ace badman of the world, got his last night—two slugs through his heart and one through his head. He was tough and he was shrewd, but he wasn't as tough and as shrewd as the Federals, who never close a case until the end. It took 27 of them to end Dillinger's career and their strength came out of his weakness—a woman.

Dillinger was put on the spot by a tipoff to the local bureau of the Department of Justice. It was a feminine voice that Melvin H. Purvis, head of the Chicago office heard. He had waited long for it.

The voice told him that Dillinger would be at a little third run movie house, the Biograph, last night—that he went there every night and usually got there about 7:30. It was almost 7:30 then. Purvis sent out a call for all the men within reach and hustled all men on hand with him. They waited more than an hour. They knew from the informer that he must come out, turn left, turn again into a dark alley where he parked his Ford-8 coupe.

Purvis himself stood at the main exit, he had men on foot and in parked inconspicuous cars strung on both sides of the alley. He was to give the signal. . . . Then the crowd that always streams out when the main picture finishes came. Purvis had seen Dillinger when he was brought through from Arizona to Crown Point, Indiana, and his heart pounded when he saw again the face that has been studied by countless millions on the front pages of the world.

Purvis gave the signal. Dillinger did not see him. Public Enemy No. 1 lit a cigarette, strolled a few feet to the alley with the mass of middle class citizens going in that direction, then wheeled left.

A Federal man, revolver in hand, stepped from behind a telegraph pole at the mouth of the passage. "Hello, John," he said, almost whispered, his voice husky with the intensity of the classic melodrama. Dillinger went with lightning right hand for his gun, a .38 Colt Automatic. He drew it from his trousers pocket.

But, from behind, another government agent thrust the muzzle of his service revolver against Dillinger's back and fired twice. Both bullets went through the bandit's heart.

He staggered, his weapon clattered to the asphalt paving, and as he went three more shots flashed. One bullet hit the back of his head, downward as he was falling and came out under his eye. . . .

Almost as sensational was the beat scored by Walter Winchell, five years later, when another underworld king, Louis "Lepke" Buchalter, boss of New York's Murder,

Inc., chose to surrender to the New York reporter, rather than the police. Lepke had supervised the murder of an estimated eighty victims in the course of his grisly career. Finally arrested for racketeering in the fur industry, he was freed by a corrupt judge and promptly jumped bail. For over three years he was high on the nation's most-wanted list. Both the F.B.I. and New York's District Attorney Thomas E. Dewey offered a reward of $25,000 for him dead or alive. Desperate, his money and power dwindling, Lepke finally decided his best hope of survival was a surrender to Winchell. His assumption: the G-men wouldn't shoot him on sight, when a newspaperman was by his side.

Winchell negotiated the surrender on the telephone, and the final arrangements were worthy of James Bond at his cold-war best. Winchell had to deal with a very jumpy and cowardly criminal and a steadily more exasperated J. Edgar Hoover, who at one point told him, "This is a lot of bunk, Walter. You are being made a fool of and so are we. If you contact those people again, tell them the time limit is up! I will instruct my agents to shoot Lepke on sight."

Winchell communicated this sentiment to Lepke's representatives and the very next night he got one more in the long succession of phone calls. This time the instructions included, "Drive up to Proctor's Theater in Yonkers."

At the theater, a man got into Winchell's car, with a handkerchief held over his face. He kept it there throughout the brief conversation. He told Winchell to go to a drugstore on the corner of 19th Street and Eighth Avenue. "There are some phone booths there. Get in one and appear busy. About 9 P.M. somebody will come up to you and tell you where to notify the G-men to meet you."

Winchell obeyed. In the drugstore, a stranger beckoned him outside. As they walked to Winchell's car, there was another muttered message. "Go back in there and tell Hoover to be at 28th Street and Fifth Avenue between 10:10 and 10:20."

Again Winchell obeyed. Back at his car, he found the man at the wheel. They drove around and around midtown Manhattan for over an hour and finally stopped in Madison Square, where his chauffeur told him, "Just wait here—and good luck."

He vanished into the night. Suddenly, Winchell wrote, "a figure approached our car in haste, out of nowhere, it seems. He opened the door, got in and said, 'Hello, thanks very much.' We released the brake and stepped on the gas. 'We'll be with Mr. Hoover in a minute or two,' we said. 'He's waiting in his car at 28th Street.'

"'Yes, I know,' said Lepke, 'I just passed him.'"

Winchell refused to accept the $25,000 reward. He gave it back as "my gift to the government." All he wanted, he said, was "a one-edition beat." Some rival reporters were infuriated by the scoop but an editorial in the Brooklyn *Eagle* maintained that Winchell had performed "an outstanding public service for which the community should be grateful." In a series of trials, mastermind Lepke was convicted of crimes ranging from narcotics smuggling to murder. He was sentenced to death and, after an all but interminable appeals to higher courts, died in the electric chair.

By now a new kind of menace was clouding the nation's

horizon. Adolf Hitler was rampaging across Europe. Once
more an American newspaperman played a brilliant role
in awakening the world to the German menace. This time
his name was Leland Stowe, and like Richard Harding
Davis in World War I, he risked his life to land in Norway
with the tiny British expeditionary force of 1500 men,
which the planners in London, for some unknown reason,
thought could halt Hitler's hordes in their 1940 conquest
of that prostrate nation. Bitterly Stowe wrote of how these
British boys were thrown into snow and mud after barely
a year's training, without anti-aircraft guns or tanks. In
four savage days, half of them were dead, wounded or
captured.

Stowe wrote of a young officer telling him, almost weeping, "We have simply been massacred. It is the planes.
We have no planes to fight back with and we have no anti-
aircraft guns. It is just like the Russians against the Finns,
only worse—and we are the Finns." Another man told
him, "We had not even got proper clothes to fight with
in the snow. Without white capes the Jerries just spotted
us and mowed us down every time the bombers drove us
out." Stowe angrily called the campaign "one of the cost-
liest and inexplicable military bungles in modern British
history." His sensational report was the final blow for
Neville Chamberlain's tottering government. The British
people realized the man who had spent his reputation on
appeasing Hitler was hardly the right leader in a war for
survival. Chamberlain retired and Winston Churchill became Prime Minister.

Other reporters, notably Quentin Reynolds and William
Shirer, told in equally vivid terms the tragic story of the

collapse of France and the heroic British resistance to Hitler's savage air attacks. Thanks to its newsmen, America was at least psychologically prepared to fight the greatest war in human history.

9. COURAGE ON LAND AND SEA

The challenge came for America at 8 A.M. on December 7, 1941. Out of the blue Sunday morning sky above Pearl Harbor came squadron after squadron of Japanese war planes to smash at the U. S. Navy ships trapped in the narrow channel below them. Frank Tremain, head of the United Press Bureau in Honolulu, was one of thousands who awoke a few minutes later, not quite believing that his windows were rattling and shivering under the impact of tremendous explosions. Tremain stumbled out of bed and blundered sleepily out of his bedroom into the living room. His house, perched high on one of Oahu's picturesque hills, looked down on the great American naval base. Blinking with unbelief through the still trembling window, Tremain watched wave after wave of Japanese planes slash at the trapped men and ships. A moment later, his equally dazed wife was by his side. The sight of her horrified face galvanized Tremain into action. "I'm going down there," he shouted. "Take a wild chance and put in a call to the UP office in San Francisco. If it comes through, tell them what you can see."

Tremain flung on some clothes and dashed for his car. A traffic jam and roadblocks by Military Police barred his route, and he never got close to the chaotic scene in the harbor. But Mrs. Tremain obeyed her newsman husband's farewell order, put in that call to the UP office in San Francisco and, amazingly, it went through. While her husband fumed on the road, she gave the wide-eyed deskmen in California an eyewitness account of the worst defeat ever suffered by the American navy.

The greatest conflict in history, the only one that truly deserved the term world war, had begun. Never before had American newsmen been faced with such a challenge. They responded with unparalleled courage and numberless feats of daring, riding the whirlwind of war around the world. Yates McDaniel of the AP fled bomb-blasted Singapore and seven days later summed up his seven-and-a-half-day journey as follows: "I abandoned a bombed ship, was cast up on an uninhabited island, made my way through a storm in a small launch to Sumatra, crossed the island's mountain wilds by truck, rail and pony cart and completed 1200 roundabout miles safely through the Indian Ocean aboard a destroyer."

For correspondents who were unlucky enough to be caught in Japan, the sneak attack on Pearl Harbor was very bad news. The Japanese regarded all foreign reporters as spies. They were dragged off to prison, questioned for hours at a time and given practically nothing to eat. Two other reporters, Robert P. Martin and William H. McDougal of the UP Bureau in Shanghai, realized that they were in trouble the moment they heard the news, and pretended to go on a drunken spree. The Japanese decided they weren't worth arresting, and they were able to escape to the safety of the Chinese lines.

Meanwhile, hundreds of other correspondents covered the fighting war. Frank Hewlett of the UP and Dean Schedler of the AP watched desperate Americans and Filipinos fight against overwhelming Japanese assaults on Bataan, and then finally retreated to the fortress island of Corregidor, in Manila Bay. On April 9, 1942, Bataan fell and everyone knew that Corregidor would soon meet the same fate. The commanding general, Jonathan Wainwright, quietly called the two correspondents to his headquarters deep in the "Rock," as Corregidor was called, and advised them to leave on two small trainer planes. They reluctantly accepted his advice, and left little more than three weeks before Corregidor surrendered. But they had stayed long enough to tell almost the full story of the heroism of its defenders—a story that inspired countless Americans to redouble their individual war efforts in the months to come.

The luckiest correspondent in these early months of the war was a forty-two-year-old Australian who had fought in World War I, become an American citizen and began writing for the Chicago *Tribune*. His name was Stanley Johnston, and after reporting German triumphs in Belgium and Holland, he was transferred to the Pacific. There, he became the only American reporter present at one of the crucial turning points of the war—the Battle of the Coral Sea. The fate of his native land, Australia, hung in the balance, and this added depth and emotion to Johnston's story. If the Japanese won, there would be nothing to stop them from launching an invasion of the subcontinent. Johnston was aboard the American aircraft carrier USS *Lexington,* and he described the epic five-day running battle, in which the two fleets never saw each other. All the deadly blows were struck with planes. The Japanese lost two irreplaceable aircraft carriers. The *Lexington* took a terrific pounding, and after desperate efforts to save her, she was finally abandoned. Johnston wrote a moving description of her last moments. "She never wavered. She kept her head up and went down like the lady she was."

Not all correspondents were as lucky as Johnston. Jack Singer, a twenty-seven-year-old INS reporter, was killed when the aircraft carrier *Wasp* took a torpedo amidships during the battle for the Solomons. Joe James Custer of the UP lost his left eye when he was struck by shell fragments from a Japanese dive bomber attack against the heavy cruiser, *Astoria.* Melville Jacoby of *Time,* who had survived the fighting on Bataan and Corregidor and escaped to Australia, was killed in a plane crash. DeWitt Hancock of the AP died when he attempted to escape from Singapore one step ahead of the triumphant Japanese, and his ship was sunk by Japanese bombers.

Narrow escapes became commonplace. Vern Haugland of the AP parachuted into the New Guinea jungle moments before his plane crashed. He survived a month of wandering in the tropic heat, living on grass and roots. But few reporters equaled Larry Allen's aptitude for survival. He persuaded the British Admiralty to let him sail aboard the cruiser *Galatea,* and thus became the first American reporter to serve aboard a British ship in wartime. The *Galatea* went down in the Mediterranean. Allen could not swim a stroke, but he clung to wreckage and was

finally rescued. His first-person story of the ordeal won him
a Pulitzer Prize. Six more times Allen went aboard ships
that were shot out from under him. The last one left him
on the beach of the enemy-held fortress city of Tobruk.
For the next twenty months, Allen was a prisoner of war.

Steadily, grimly, the Allies took the offensive. First came
the invasion of North Africa. UP correspondent Leon
Disher stood on the bridge of the American Coast Guard
cutter *Walney* as it steamed into the harbor of Oran. Vichy
French artillery opened up, and a direct hit on the bridge
killed everyone but Disher. He leaped off the sinking
ship, badly wounded in both legs. French machine gunners
blasted away at survivors floundering in the water.
Wounded an unbelievable twenty-six times, Disher never-
theless made it to shore, and lived.

While the Germans and the Americans fought in North
Africa, an even more important battle was roaring to a
climax in the Russian industrial city of Stalingrad. Strict
Moscow censorship would not let American reporters anywhere near the fighting, until it was clear that the Russian
armies had surrounded the Germans and victory was certain. Henry Shapiro of the UP rushed to the scene, the
moment permission was given. He found among the Russian officers and soldiers "an air of confidence the like
of which I had never seen in the Red Army before." When
he returned to Moscow, he dramatically informed his
American readers, "The Germans are doomed." Less than
two months later, the 91,000 German survivors of the
330,000-man Sixth Army surrendered.

Other reporters gave Americans eyewitness descriptions
of the massive Allied bombing raids over Germany. Walter

Cronkite of the UP, flying on a raid over Wilhelmshaven on February 26, 1943, said it was "an assignment to hell—a hell 26,000 feet above the earth, a hell of burning tracer bullets and bursting gunfire, of crippled fortresses and burning German fighter planes, of parachuting men and others not so lucky." One of his fellow reporters, Robert P. Post of the New York *Times,* was among the not so lucky.

In the Mediterranean, John H. Thompson, military editor of the Chicago *Tribune,* jumped into Sicily with the 505th Regiment of the 82nd Airborne Division. It was a night drop and the planes scattered their human cargo over eighty miles of the island. Thompson landed in a tree, injuring his knee and then groped through the darkness for the rest of the night, finally joining the regiment's commander, Colonel James Gavin, in time to watch the paratroopers fight off a German tank counterattack. Thompson rushed to a nearby airstrip, zoomed back to North Africa aboard the first U.S. plane to land in Sicily, and fired off the first eyewitness account of the Sicilian invasion, which included the happy news that the German radio report of the "annihilation" of the United States paratroopers was highly exaggerated.

Thompson's story arrived at the *Tribune*'s desk while the managing editor and another reporter friend were walking up and down in front of his apartment, trying to get up courage to go in and tell his wife that he was either dead or a prisoner. They decided to wait one more day and returned to find the good news of his survival— plus a sensational beat—waiting on the cable desk.

That night the *Tribune* sent Thompson a bonus, plus an order: "Jump no more."

One of the most harrowing stories of the war was covered by George E. Jones of the United Press, a reporter who had been in so many island invasions in the South Pacific that he was called "First Wave" Jones. This time, however, Jones was not storming a beach. On October 23, 1944, he was aboard the aircraft carrier *Lexington* at the elbow of Vice Admiral Marc A. Mitscher during the forty-eight hours of nonstop battle off the Philippines that destroyed the Japanese home fleet. For Jones it was like watching a gigantic chess game on a movie screen. He could ponder the strategy of the opposing admirals, almost as if he was not involved, watching the various groups of ships jockeying for position, while planes, submarines and destroyers darted in to attack and retreat. When it was over, Jones began his historic story:

> Today the Japanese fleet submitted itself to the destinies of war—and lost.
> Four enemy carriers have been sunk. Eight battleships have been damaged . . . a total of 25 Japanese ships have gone to the bottom.

Jones narrated the heroic fight of a group of small American carriers against a vastly more powerful Japanese squadron, described heavy air attacks on the *Lexington*, and the intricate maneuvers of the thirty vessels in task force 38, while Japanese bombs and Kamikaze planes poured from the skies.

But the reporter who won the greatest reputation in World War II did not write about war in heroic terms, nor did he hesitate to admit that he himself was frequently

terrified by the constant danger of death which reporters
and soldiers alike faced. His name was Ernie Pyle, and he
was the total opposite of the trench-coated hero reporter
in the Richard Harding Davis style. A wizened little man
who seldom weighed more than 110 pounds and was
almost bald, Pyle became the idol of GIs because he
told the story of the war the way they experienced it. He
communicated both their heroism and their loneliness, their
bravery and their boredom. "I love the infantry because
they are the underdogs," Pyle wrote. "They are the mud-
rain-frost-and-wind boys. They have no comforts and they
even learn to live without the necessities. And in the end
they are the guys that wars can't be won without." Watching a column of infantrymen trudging across the barren
North African hills, he wrote,

> They don't slouch. It is the terrible deliberation of each
> step that spells out their appalling tiredness. Their faces are
> black and unshaved. They are young men, but the grime
> and whiskers and exhaustion make them look middle-
> aged. . . .
> There is an agony in your heart and you feel almost
> ashamed to look at them. They are just guys from Broadway
> and Main Street, but maybe you wouldn't remember them.
> They are too far away now. They are too tired.

In a place called Shell Alley, on the Anzio beachhead in
Italy, Pyle missed death by inches. Outside Naples, artillery
fire killed three other reporters with whom he had been
working. After ten days under fire in France, he confessed:
"I'm so sick of living in misery and fright."

Still he kept on taking risks. When the American First
Army was within a hundred miles of Paris, Pyle and three
other reporters boldly asked for permission to move ahead
of the army and enter the city unescorted. They were
refused. Several other correspondents, led by Ernest Hemingway, broke the rules and drove ahead anyway. Pyle
stayed with his GIs and described their entry into the
French capital. "We all got kissed until we were literally
red in the face, and I must say we enjoyed it. . . . The
fact that I hadn't shaved for days and was grey bearded as
well as bald headed, made no difference." Then, with his
total honesty, Pyle testified to the terrible strain of more
than a year in the front lines. "All of a sudden it seemed
to me that if I heard one more shot or saw one more dead
man I would go off my nut and if I had to write one more
column I'd collapse."

The little man went home for a rest. But he could not
stay away from the fighting front. In a few months he
went out to the Pacific to write about other GI Joes, fighting
a jungle war. But in spirit, he was beside Americans wherever they were fighting. When the news of the German
surrender reached him, he sat down and wrote: "My heart
is still in Europe and that's why I am writing this column.
It is to the boys who were my friends for so long. My one
great regret of the war is that I am not with them when it
has ended. For the companionship of two and a half years
of death and misery is a spouse that tolerates no divorce."

Ernie Pyle stuck this half-finished column in his pocket
and went ashore with men from the 77th Division attacking
the island of Ie Shima. A hidden Japanese machine gun suddenly opened up and everyone dived into the nearest ditch.

Pyle raised his head to see if anyone was hit, and three
bullets killed him instantly. On the site of his death the GIs
placed a small inscription.

AT THIS SPOT

THE

77TH INFANTRY DIVISION

LOST A BUDDY

ERNIE PYLE

Overall throughout the war 37 newsmen died under
enemy attack and 112 were wounded—a casualty rate
about four times higher than the fighting forces. Along
with the staggering 1646 accredited correspondents repre-
senting American newspapers, magazines and radio stations
there were hundreds of combat correspondents from *Stars
and Stripes,* the soldiers' newspaper, and *Yank,* the GI
magazine.

Compared to World War I, there was far less difficulty
with government censorship. American officials did their
best to let correspondents cover the war as freely as possible.
Their copy was still subject to the censor's scrutiny, but only
information that was deemed secret or of possible aid to
the enemy was deleted. One correspondent who ran into
serious trouble was Stanley Johnston of Coral Sea fame. He
described the Japanese battle fleet at Midway in such detail, U.S. officials feared that the enemy might realize that
the United States had broken the Japanese secret code. A
federal grand jury investigated Johnston, but he was ex-
onerated of any intentional wrongdoing. In Moscow, Harrison Salisbury of the United Press got into even hotter

water with the Russians when a UP man in London wrote a story about Stalin hitting Marshal Semyon Timoshenko over the head with a bottle during a party for Winston Churchill. Only a formal apology by the United Press saved Salisbury from expulsion.

Finally, American, Russian and British armies pounded Hitler's fortress Europa into rubble, the Fuehrer committed suicide in his Berlin bunker, and Germany surrendered. To a world that was more inclined to celebrate than listen to more bad news, correspondents began telling the story of the Nazi death camps. From Buchenwald, Auschwitz, Maidanek and other murder factories, reporters told unbelieving readers how Hitler's *Einsatzgruppen* had killed six million Jews and millions of other helpless people. It was a story the world had to know and the correspondents piled it on, determined that no one would ever look fondly back on Hitler and his thugs and see through a sentimental haze a noble lost cause.

In the Pacific, a few months later, a gifted reporter described another more ominous ending to that phase of the war. William Leonard Laurence of the New York *Times* had been drafted by Major General Leslie Groves to handle all the press information in connection with the building of the atomic bomb. Yet for well over a year, he could not write a word about it publicly. Then, with sealed orders, Laurence flew to the Pacific. He thought he was to witness the first atomic bomb, which was dropped on Hiroshima. For some unexplained reason, he missed that flight. But four days later, he was permitted to go aboard one of the two B-29s that accompanied the strike bomber "The Great Artiste," which dropped the second atomic bomb on Nagasaki. For the first time, a professional reporter described the world's most fearsome weapon.

Out of the belly of The Great Artiste what looked like a black object went downward. . . . A giant flash broke through the dark barrier of our arc welder's lenses and flooded our cabin with intense light.

A tremendous blast wave struck our ship and made it tremble from nose to tail. This was followed by four more blasts in rapid succession, each resounding like the boom of cannon fire hitting our plane from all directions.

Observers in the tail of our ship saw a giant ball of fire rise as though from the bowels of the earth, belching forth enormous white smoke rings. Next they saw a giant pillar of purple fire ten thousand feet high, shooting skyward with enormous speed. . . .

Less than a month later, Japan surrendered. Among the witnesses on the deck of the USS *Missouri* were two hundred Allied reporters. Even before this formal end of the war, newsmen such as Homer Bigart of the New York *Herald Tribune* had gone ashore and visited the ruins of Hiroshima. He reported "flat, appalling desolation, the starkness accentuated by bare blackened tree trunks and the occasional shell of a reinforced concrete building." Survivors were still "dying at the rate of about 100 daily." Once more, newsmen were forcing their readers to face a difficult truth—men had created a weapon capable of destroying civilization.

The message became all the more important in the years to come. The wartime alliance swiftly broke up, and the Russian Communists unmasked their virulent hatred and suspicion of the free societies of America and Western Europe. It was not long before a veteran newsman, Herbert Bayard Swope, coined a term to describe this strange new international conflict. It was, he said, a cold war.

10. ON THE JOB AROUND THE WORLD

The scene was somewhere in Korea. The Communists had broken through and American and South Korean soldiers were retreating. At dawn, as the long lines of weary men slogged toward the rear, they were suddenly electrified by an amazing sight. An American woman, dressed in a navy blue skirt, flowered blouse and bright blue sweater, had a typewriter perched on the hood of a stalled jeep and was pounding away on it.

Maggie Higgins, America's best-known female reporter, was hard at work. Her tireless persistence and daring were not unusual—except for the fact that she was a woman. In fact, Maggie Higgins was always quick to point out that she was doing no more than dozens of other reporters to alert America to the harsh facts of a bitterly divided post-war world.

Newsmen had been warning Americans of mounting tension between the Communist and free worlds long before Marguerite Higgins came to Korea. "There are no new ideas in Moscow," Brooks Atkinson wrote in the New York *Times,* reluctantly informing a bewildered America that their wartime ally, Russia, had succumbed to communism's old dream of world domination. In the New York *Herald Tribune*, John Steinbeck made the dimensions of the threat even more menacing by describing in shocking detail the tyrannical reign of Joseph Stalin. "We doubt whether even Augustus Caesar had during his lifetime the . . . hold on his people that Stalin has."

Thanks to such unmistakable warnings, Americans soon realized that they were involved in a new and often confusing war for survival. It was a war that might explode into violence at any moment—and explode it did, on a practically unknown Asian peninsula named Korea.

With angry, unbelieving eyes, Maggie Higgins and three other correspondents watched the first Americans go into action against the Communists. The Americans were using out-of-date World War II weapons. Their bazooka shells simply bounced off the Reds' new armor-plated tanks. In a few minutes, the Americans still unhurt were running for their lives. Maggie and her fellow reporters made sure this alarming news got back to America, fast.

When the Communists began their assault, there were only five American correspondents in Korea. Within a week, there were seventy on the job, ducking shells and bullets, and getting the news out somehow, as the Americans and South Koreans continued their headlong retreat. By September 1950—three months after the fighting began —there were 238 accredited correspondents in the war.

It was an exhausting, very dangerous war. Communist troops were everywhere, disguised as farmers, Buddhist priests, even as women. Most reporters began carrying guns.

"The main difference between a newsman and a soldier

in Korea," Maggie Higgins wrote, "was that a soldier in combat had to get out of his hole and go after the enemy, whereas the correspondent had the privilege of keeping his head down. It was commonplace for correspondents to be at the company and platoon level, and many of us frequently went on patrol. We felt it was the only honest way of covering the war. The large number of correspondents killed or captured in Korea is testimony of the dangers to which scores willingly subjected themselves."

When American paratroopers jumped behind Red lines, Bob Vermillion of the UP plummeted earthward with them. With a broken ankle, he gimped back to the American lines and got his story out via field telephone. When the First Marine Division was trapped near Chongin Reservoir, deep in wintry North Korea, Keyes Beech of the Chicago *Daily News* volunteered to join it. A veteran of Tarawa and Iwo Jima in World War II, he told Americans that he had never seen men suffer so much, so stoically. "The wonder isn't that they fought their way out against overwhelming odds," he wrote, "but that they were able to survive the cold and fight at all."

But if the war had a star reporter, it was Maggie Higgins. She won the title, however, not because she was a woman, but because she insisted on covering the war where it was happening, in the front lines. To stay there, Maggie had to survive both the Communists' and the American army's prejudice against female reporters. After surviving the harrowing retreat from South Korea's capital down the peninsula to Pusan, Maggie thought she had more than earned her right to a front-line assignment. Instead, she got an order from the commanding American general, Walton

H. Walker, sending her back to Japan. "There are no facilities at the front for ladies," he declared. Walker soon found himself with a very infuriated lady on his hands. Maggie appealed over his head to Supreme Commander Douglas MacArthur. He gave her permission to stay in Korea.

Maggie Higgins later suggested that the real reason for Walker's order was her refusal to doctor her stories about the first grim weeks of fighting in Korea. In reply, she insisted on the importance of the truth. "It is best to admit panic among our soldiers and so bring home the great need for better training. It is best to admit that bazookas don't even tickle the big Soviet tanks and make known the urgent need for better and more weapons; it is best to tell graphically the moments of desperation and horror endured by an unprepared army, so that the American public will demand that it will not happen again."

A few weeks later, Maggie was with an American unit that was surrounded and almost cut off by a Communist surprise attack. As bullets buzzed through paper-thin walls and casualties streamed into the emergency hospital, she joined the medics. "One correspondent learned to administer blood plasma," she wrote in her story of the incident. The colonel of the regiment, Mike Michaelis, saw the story and wrote a letter to Maggie's paper, accusing her of gross understatement. He described in vivid detail the help she had given the wounded.

Maggie had two reactions to the letter. "That Mike Michaelis should take time out from a war to write that letter was deeply moving to me. I treasure that letter beyond anything that has happened to me in Korea, or anywhere." That was Maggie Higgins, the woman, talking. Then the reporter added: "After the publication of that letter it was hard for headquarters generals to label me a nuisance and use it as an excuse for restricting my activities."

While hot war boiled in Asia, other reporters fought the cold war in Europe. On April 26, 1951, the Communists seized William N. Oatis of the AP and sentenced him to ten years in prison, as a spy. Correspondent after correspondent was hounded out or expelled from Russia until finally the U.S. press corps in Moscow consisted of three men, who hung on, enduring the constant spying and harassment. When he finally came home, Harrison Salisbury wrote: "I was more than happy to leave . . . a country where I had known the chill of terror, the shadow of suspicion and the blackness of tragedy."

Korea sputtered to a close. Then came an explosion that rocked the Communist world—the Hungarian revolution of 1956. The only American correspondent in Budapest, Russell Jones of the UP, stayed to the bitter end of this abortive bid for freedom. Watching the Russian tanks and shells smash the beautiful city to rubble, he wrote, "For the first time since I was a boy I wept." The Russians finally expelled Jones for telling too much of the truth. When he got to London, he summed up what he had seen in a final story which won him the Pulitzer Prize for International Reporting.

WHY BUDAPEST FOUGHT

London, Dec. 10—The greatest shock to the Hungarian Communists and their Russian masters must have been the type of people who fought the hardest.

Believe none of the stories that this was a misguided
uprising fomented to restore the great estate owners of the
Horthy regency or the industrial magnates. I saw with my
own eyes who was fighting and heard with my ears why
they fought.

The first armed resistance came from students of the
schools and universities, the youth who had been so carefully
selected as the party elite of the future.

The fiercest fighters were the workers, the proletarians
in whose name Communism had ruled. Even the Hungarian
army, purged and repurged a dozen times, joined the
battle for freedom or sat on the sidelines.

The two big names that came out of the revolt were
Communist—Imre Nagy, a lifelong party member, and
Lieutenant Colonel Pal Maleter, who had deserted to the
Russians in World War II and returned as a Red partisan.

Wherever came the spark, it found its tinder among the
common people.

The areas of destruction, the buildings most desperately
defended and the dead themselves are the most eloquent
proof of this. It was the workers' tenements that Soviet
siege guns smashed, factory buildings that became forts and
the tired shabby men with broken shoes and horny hands
of the laborer who died by the thousands. The women with
their hair bound with kerchiefs and the cheap and tawdry
dresses of working people.

A seventeen-year-old girl, twice wounded at Corvin
Theatre, told me she fought because "it isn't right that my
father with four children to feed should get only 900 florints
[$80] a month."

The chairman of the Workers' Council at the Csepel
Iron and Steel plant with 38,000 workers, biggest in the
country, said, "These are our factories. We will fight to

the death to hold them. But we will continue plant maintenance because we want to work here again."

In Dorog, one of the coal centers, miners continued to work despite the general strike. But not to produce coal. They didn't want their mines ruined by flooding.

The same attitude is taken in the country. The farmers want to get out of the collectives but they do not want the restoration of the landlords. They think everyone should have the right to own and till his own land. Something like 100 acres a family would be fair, they think.

It was for these simple, basic things that the Hungarian people fought. These and the right to speak, think freely, to elect men of their own choice, and to raise their children in their own way.

They will go on fighting for them.

Then Cuba began to bubble. Herbert L. Matthews of the New York *Times* slogged into the Cuban hills to interview an obscure guerrilla named Fidel Castro, who at that point had exactly eighteen soldiers and was completely surrounded by the Cuban army. In a style that was something of a throwback to Richard Harding Davis, Matthews wrote, "This is the first sure news that Fidel Castro is still alive and still in Cuba. . . . No one in Havana, not even at the United States Embassy with all its resources for getting information, will know until this report is published that Fidel Castro is really in the Sierra Maestra."

Unfortunately, Matthews came away convinced that Castro was not a Communist and from this initial blunder the whole American press experience with Cuba has been one of the few blots on American reporting in the cold-war era.

But Cuba dwindled in importance as the United States became involved in Vietnam. In this, the most frustrating and confusing of all American wars, the press has played a unique role. U.S. reporters, notably Malcolm Brown of the AP, Neil Sheean of the UPI and David Halberstam of the New York *Times,* actually changed the policies of the United States Government by grimly insisting in their stories that the war was being lost when U.S. officials were claiming an imminent victory.

As the conflict escalated to a limited but terribly lethal war, American reporters once more joined the troops in the field, sharing the risks of the fighting men. Maggie Higgins came home to die a slow painful death from an obscure Asian disease. A younger woman correspondent, Philippa Schuyler, who gave up a career as a concert pianist to go to Vietnam, was helping to evacuate children from the town of Hue when she was killed in a helicopter crash. Ron Gallagher, a twenty-nine-year-old free-lance correspondent, died when U.S. artillery fire fell short outside Saigon. One of his papers, the Fort Scott *Tribune,* wrote of him: "He had something to say that he wanted to get across to a fence straddling country about the importance of Vietnam. He said it well, he died saying it." Bernard Fall, perhaps the most knowledgeable writer on Vietnam, with seven books to his credit, was killed instantly when he stepped on a Viet Cong land mine.

On the other side of the world, other newsmen fought a more peaceful, but no less bitter, cold-war battle in Sweden. English philosopher Bertrand Russell organized a "War Crimes Trial" in Stockholm, as part of the Communist propaganda campaign against the United States war effort

in Vietnam. Two U.S. reporters, Gordon McLendon and
Don W. Burden, covering the proceedings for UPI and
broadcasting outlets, wrote "less than complimentary" stories. They were particularly suspicious of the other so-called
reporters on the scene and began taking pictures of the
press gallery. "It was the first time I ever saw a newspaperman reluctant to have his picture taken," McLendon says.
"There were about two hundred 'newsmen' in the large
auditorium. As we looked at them, we saw girls in mini-
skirts and men with hair to their shoulders. . . . There
were only twenty to twenty-five responsible journalists there,
and the rest were Swedish students."

Burden and McLendon were told it was "not permissible"
to take pictures of these strange journalists. When they per-
sisted, they were expelled from the trial. Their expulsion
revealed to the world the rigged, Communist-backed nature
of the trial. "It received heavy exposure in the European
press for two days," McLendon says.

Little more than a month later, while Vietnam's reporters
continued to risk death in the ambush-filled jungle, other
newsmen rode jeeps and trucks into the Sinai desert to
report the brief, fierce renewal of war between Israel and
the Arab states.

Serge Fliegers, of Hearst Headline Service, who had
covered the fighting on the same battlefields in 1956, rode
into the Egyptian stronghold of Gaza in a rented car with
Ben Oyserman, a cameraman for the Canadian Broadcasting Company. In 1956, Fliegers had been one of the
first correspondents into Gaza. "The last time I got away
with just a story," he says. "This time I got the story, but I
paid the price—the price every correspondent may have to

pay sometime, somewhere in this troubled world." An Egyptian mine exploded only a few yards away, killing Oyserman, and shredding Fliegers' legs and face with shrapnel.

Hugh Mulligan of AP, who had already distinguished himself as a reporter in Vietnam, spent harrowing hours in an Israeli kibbutz under intense Syrian mortar fire, waiting for an anticipated assault that would have certainly wiped out the handful of defenders. Israeli tanks rescued them. Others were not so lucky. Paul Schutzer, whose camera had recorded the building of the Berlin Wall, the Algerian war and other stories, was killed by an Egyptian shell in the Gaza strip.

On the home front in the postwar era, the American newspaper has continued to publish the news of a turbulent, changing American nation and a chaotic world. Reporters continued to fight corruption wherever they found it. Mrs. Caro Brown of the Alice, Texas, *Daily Echo* wrote a series of stories that toppled the one-man political empire of George B. Parr, the Duke of Duvall County. In Chicago, a reader's tip led another tough reporter, George Thyen, to the story of how the state auditor had looted $2,500,000 from the city treasury.

At the same time, along with the news, a new kind of reporter was emerging—the interpretive specialist who put the news in perspective. One of the best was Austin C. Wehrwein, whose series of articles on Canada in 1952 explained the subtle differences between Americans and their neighbors to the north. Other reporters summoned Americans to ponder the problems of urban sprawl, the "metro city" of the imminent future. This was one of newspapers' many responses to television and radio coverage of spot news, which deluged the listener with information, with little or no attempt to make it comprehensible.

Elsewhere, newspapers have developed a growing sensitivity for the rights and needs of the individual in our increasingly mass society. Edwin O. Guthman of the Seattle *Times* spent five months in 1950 digging out facts that cleared a University of Washington professor of charges that he was a Communist. Anthony Lewis of the Washington *Daily News* took on the entire Navy Department to find out why an obscure employee named Abraham Chasanow was fired as a security risk on April 7, 1954. Thanks to his reporting, a new hearing board found that Chasanow was "an above-average loyal American citizen with long creditable service for the government."

When Ralph L. Lowenstein of the El Paso *Times* heard of a Mexican family that was living on two sides of the border because the mother had been deported by the United States Immigration and Naturalization Service under a heartlessly strict interpretation of the Immigration Act of 1952, he wrote a Mother's Day feature story describing the family's plight. The father, a $48-a-week laborer, lived in a one-room apartment in El Paso with the couple's four oldest daughters. The mother lived in a one-room apartment in Juarez, Mexico, with their three youngest daughters. The paper ran four more articles on similarly separated families. The result was a ruling from the Commissioner of United States Immigration, permitting the Valadez family and three hundred other families to be reunited in the first year and hundreds more in succeeding years. No longer did the Immigration service coldly divide

families. Compassion became a basic word in their administration of the law.

The 1969 Pulitzer prizes testified to the continuing
vitality of this newspaper tradition. Winners of prizes for
local reporting were Albert L. Delugach and Denny Walsh
of the St. Louis *Globe-Democrat* for a three-year-long series
of articles that exposed fraud and abuse of power within
the St. Louis Steamfitters Union, Local 562. Three of the
union's officers were convicted on charges of conspiracy to
violate laws against the use of union funds in federal
election campaigns.

Another Pulitzer Prize for local reporting went to John
Fedderman of the Louisville, Kentucky, *Courier Journal*
for a simply told moving account of a soldier's burial in
rural Kentucky. The article began, "It was late on a
Wednesday night when most of the people were asleep in
Hindman, the county seat of Knott County, when the body
of Private First Class James (Little Duck) Gibson came
home from Vietnam. . . ." In clear, compassionate prose,
Mr. Fedderman demonstrated once more the newspaper's
power to dramatize the lives of obscure individuals, and
also to bring home to readers the meaning of the melancholy
statistics of the Vietnam War, with its 30,000 American
dead.

Still another aspect of the newspaper's long reach was
the Pulitzer Prize won by Robert Cahn, a Washington
correspondent for the *Christian Science Monitor*. With a
photographer he traveled twenty thousand miles, visited
more than twenty national parks from Florida to the state
of Washington to make a searching report on how these

vital islands of natural beauty were surviving the pressures of increased public use.

Obviously, American newspapermen have not forgotten that they are members of the only profession in the country given special protection by virtue of the First Amendment. More than any other single group of men, they are the watchmen of the American republic, committed by their profession to the difficult and often dangerous task of safeguarding the values by which the American nation lives. May they continue to remain faithful to their great tradition.

INDEX

Adams, John, 4, 5
Adams, Maude, 87
Adams, Samuel, 4
Albany *Register*, 21
Alice, Texas, *Daily Echo*, 128
Allen, Larry, 109–10
Anderson, Robert, 42
Antietam, battle of, 40
Arab states, 127–28
Argus of Western America, The,
    25, 26
Associated Press (AP). *See* spe-
    cific correspondents
Astoria, USS, 109
Atkinson, Brooks, 119–20
Atomic bomb, 116–17
Australia, 108

Bache, Ben Franklin, 17
Baltimore, Md., 15, 16
Baltimore *Federal Republican*,
    20
Bataan, 108
Beauregard, Pierre, 39
Beech, Keyes, 121
Belgium, 79–81
Benjamin, Anna Northend, 72
Bennett, James Gordon, 28–32,
    38

Bennett, James Gordon, Jr.,
    56–57
Bigart, Homer, 117
Billings, Warren, 93
Blackwell's Island, 62
Blair, Francis P., 25–26
Bly, Nellie, 61–64
Bohemian Brigade, 39–53
Boston, Mass., 2, 4
Boston *Courant*, 5–6
Bradford, Andrew, 9
Brooklyn, USS, 76, 77
Brooklyn *Eagle*, 103
Broun, Heywood, 86
Brown, Caro, 128
Brussels, 80–81
Buchalter, Louis "Lepke," 101–3
Burden, Don W., 127
Burnside, Ambrose, 41
Burr, Aaron, 20, 21–25
Byers, William Newton, 59
Byington, Homer, 47

Cahn, Robert, 130–31
Calhoun, John C., 26
California, 37, 93
Canada, 128
Capone, Al, 100
Castro, Fidel, 125

Censorship, 82, 84–85, 87–88, 115–16. *See also* specific subjects
Cervera, Pasqual, 76
Chamberlain, Neville, 104
Charleston, S.C., 16, 38–39
Chasanow, Abraham, 129
Chicago, Ill., 37, 100–1, 128
Chicago *Daily News*, 95–97, 121
Chicago *Record*, 69
Chicago *Tribune*, 37, 70, 108, 111
Christian Science Monitor, 130–31
Churchill, Winston, 104
Cincinnati *Gazette*, 46–47
Cincinnati *Philanthropist*, 36
Cisneros, Evangelina, 67
Civil War, 38–53
Clay, Henry, 26
Clemenceau, Georges, 88
Cobbett, William, 17
Cold Harbor, battle of, 51–52
Collins, Floyd, 97–99
Connolly, Richard B., 55, 56
Constitution, U.S., 17
Coral Sea, battle of, 108–9
Corregidor, 108
Cosby, William, 10–12
Crane, Stephen, 71, 73–74
Creelman, James, 71, 74–76
"Crisis, The," 14
Cronkite, Walter, 110–11
Croswell, Harry, 18
Cuba, 66–67, 68–69, 71–77, 125
Custer, Joe James, 109

Darrow, Clarence, 97
Davis, Jefferson, 44
Davis, Richard Harding, 72–73, 77, 78–82

Dawes, William, 3
Death camps, Nazi, 116
Delugach, Albert L., 130
De Quille, Don, 60
Dewey, George, 69–70
Dewey, Thomas E., 102
Dill, Benjamin Franklin, 45
Dillinger, John, 100–1
Disher, Leon, 110
Dunning, John P., 76

Edes, Benjamin, 4
El Caney, 74–76
El Paso *Times*, 129

Fall, Bernard, 126
Farragut, David, 42ff.
Fedderman, John, 130
Federalist party, 16, 17
Ferguson, Fred, 88
Fliegers, Serge, 127–28
Fontaine, Felix Gregory De, 38–39
Forrest, Wilbur, 83
Fort Henry, 41
Fort Scott *Tribune*, 126
Fort Sumter, 38–39, 42
France, 87–88ff., 114
Frankfort, Ky., *Western World*, 20
Franklin, Benjamin, 5–10, 11
Franklin, Deborah, 10
Franklin, James, 5
Franks, Bobby, 95–97
Fredericksburg, battle of, 40–41
Freedom of the press, 17–19

Galatea, USS, 109
Gallagher, Ron, 126
Gas, poison, 83
Gavin, James, 111
Gaza, 127–28

George III, 4
Germany. *See* World War I; World War II
Gettysburg, battle of, 46–47
Gibbons, Floyd, 84, 85–86
Gibson, Charles Dana, 78
Gibson, James, 130
Gill, John, 4
Gloucester, USS, 76
Goddard, Mary, 15
Goddard, William, 15–16
Goldstein, Alvin H., 95–97
Graham, George, 76, 77
Grant, Ulysses S., 47ff.
Great Britain, 104. *See also* Revolutionary War
Greeley, Horace, 28–29, 32–35, 39
Grey, Francis, 46
Groves, Leslie, 116
Guthman, Edwin O., 129

Hamilton, Alexander, 16, 17–18, 21–25
Hamilton, Andrew, 11–12
Hancock, DeWitt, 109
Hancock, John, 4
Harden, Edwin W., 69
Harper's Weekly, 56
Harriet Lane, USS, 42
Harrison, Charlie, 59
Haugland, Vern, 109
Havana, 68–69
Hearst, William Randolph, 64ff., 71, 76–77
Hemingway, Ernest, 114
Heney, Francis J., 93
Henry, Patrick, 4
Herschel, Sir John, 35
Hewlett, Frank, 108
Higgins, Marguerite, 119–23, 126
Hiroshima, 116, 117

Hitler, Adolf, 104, 116
Hooker, Joseph, 40
Hoover, J. Edgar, 102, 103
Howard, Roy, 90–91
Hudson, N.Y., *Wasp*, 18
Humboldt, Baron Alexander von, 19
Hungary, 123–25

Ie Shima, 114–15
International News Service (INS). *See* specific correspondents
Irwin, Will, 83
Israel, 127–28

Jackson, Andrew, 25–26, 27
Jacoby, Melville, 109
Japan, 106–9, 115ff.
Jefferson, Thomas, 16, 17, 18–19, 20
Jewett, Helen, 30
Joffre, Joseph, 86
Johnson, Hiram, 93
Johnston, Stanley, 108–9, 115
Jones, George, 55
Jones, George E., 112
Jones, Russell, 123–25
"Journalism in Tennessee," 20–21

Kansas City *Evening Star*, 56
Kelly's Ford, 48
Kendall, Amos, 26
King, Thomas S., 59
"Kitchen Cabinet," 26
Korea, 119–23

Laconia, SS, 84
Lait, Jack, 100–1
Laurence, William Leonard, 116–17
Lee, Charles, 15

Lee, Robert E., 40, 44, 52, 53
Leopold, Nathan F., 96–97
Lewis, Anthony, 129
Lexington, battle of, 1–4
Lexington, USS, 109, 112
Lincoln, Abraham, 37, 44, 47, 50–51, 52
Litchfield, Conn., *Inquirer,* 52
Livingstone, David, 57–58
Loeb, Richard, 95–97
Louisville, Ky., *Courier Journal,* 97–99, 130
Louvain, 81
Lovejoy, Elijah P., 36
Lowell, James Russell, 53
Lowenstein, Ralph L., 129
Lusitania, SS, 83

MacArthur, Douglas, 122
McCutcheon, John T., 69
McDaniel, Yates, 107
McDougal, William H., 107–8
McGowan, Ned, 59
McKinley, William, 67, 70
McLendon, Gordon, 127
Maine, USS, 67, 68–69
Martin, Robert P., 107–8
Maryland *Gazette,* 15–16
Mason, George, 17
Massachusetts, 1–6
Massachusetts *Spy,* 1–3
Mata Hari, 88–89
Matthews, Herbert L., 125
Medill, Joseph, 37
Memphis *Appeal,* 45
Mexico; Mexicans, 79, 84, 129–30
Michaelis, Mike, 122–23
Midway, battle of, 115
Miller, "Skeets," 97–99
Missouri, USS, 117
Mitscher, Marc A., 112

Mooney, Tom, 93–95
Mott, Frank Luther, 45
Mulligan, Hugh, 128
Mulroy, James W., 95–97

Nagasaki, 117
Nast, Thomas, 56
National Intelligencer. See Washington *National Intelligencer*
National parks, 130–31
Nelson, William Rockhill, 56
New Jersey *Gazette,* 15
New Orleans, La., 42–44
New York (city), 10–12, 16, 28–36, 55–56
New York (state), 18, 62
New York *Evening Post,* 22–25
New York *Herald,* 29–32, 38–39, 42ff., 57–58. *See also* specific correspondents
New York *Herald Tribune,* 117, 120
New York *Journal,* 65–67
New York *Morning Chronicle,* 21–22
New York *Sun,* 35–36
New York *Times,* 39, 55–56, 89. *See also* specific correspondents
New York *Tribune,* 32–35, 39–40ff., 54–55
New York *Weekly Journal,* 10–12
New York *Weekly Tribune,* 33
New York *World,* 46, 62–64, 66, 70. *See also* specific correspondents
North Africa, 110, 113, 127–28
Norway, 104

Oatis, William N., 123

O'Brien, James, 55
Older, Fremont, 92–95
Olympia, USS, 69
Osbon, B. S., 42–44
Otis, James, 4
Oxman, Frank, 93
Oyserman, Ben, 127–28

Paine, Thomas, 14
Paris, 114
Parr, George B., 128
Paul Pry, 61
Pearl Harbor, 106–7
Penn, William, 9
Pennsylvania, 6–10
Pennsylvania *Evening Post and Daily Advertiser*, 16
Pennsylvania *Freeman*, 36
Pennsylvania *Gazette*, 6–9
Pennsylvania *Journal*, 14
Pennsylvania *Mercury*, 9
Pennsylvania *Packet and Daily Advertiser*, 16
Pershing, John J., 85, 86
Philadelphia, 6–9, 16. *See also* Pennsylvania *Freeman*
Philippines, 108; Manila, 69–70
Pickett's charge, 46–47
Porcupine's Gazette, 17
Post, Robert P., 111
Princeton, N.J., 14–15
Proprietary party, 9
Pulitzer, Joseph, 62, 64–65, 65–66
Pulitzer prizes, 130–31
Purvis, Melvin H., 100–1
Pyle, Ernie, 113–15

Ram (Confederate ship), 43
Raymond, Henry, 39
Rea, George Bronson, 68–69
Reid, Whitelaw, 46–47, 54–55

Republican party, 16–17
Revere, Paul, 2, 3–4
Revolutionary War, 1–4, 6, 13–16
Reynolds, Quentin, 104
Richardson, Albert B., 41–42
Richmond *Inquirer*, 27
Rivington, James, 13
Roosevelt, Theodore, 72–73
Rough Riders, 72–73
Royal Gazette, 13
Royall, Ann, 61
Ruef, Abe, 92–93
Runyon, Damon, 85
Russell, Bertrand, 126
Russia, 110, 115–16, 117–18, 123

Sacramento *Phoenix*, 59
St. Louis *Democrat*, 56
St. Louis *Globe-Democrat*, 130
St. Louis *Observer*, 36
St. Louis *Post-Dispatch*, 64–65
St. Mihiel, 88
Salisbury, Harrison, 115–16, 123
San Francisco, Calif., 92–93
San Francisco *Bulletin*, 59, 92–94
San Francisco *Call*, 94
San Francisco *Examiner*, 65
Schedler, Dean, 108
Schley, Winfield S., 76
Schmitts, Eugene, 93
Schutzer, Paul, 128
Schuyler, Philippa, 126
Scovel, Sylvester, 68–69
Seattle *Times*, 129
Serle, Ambrose, 13
Shapiro, Henry, 110
Sherman, William Tecumseh, 41
Shirer, William, 104
Sicily, 111

Singer, Jack, 109
Slavery, 34–35, 36
Smalley, George, 40
Smith, Samuel Harrison, 19–20
Spanish-American War, 66–67, 68–77
Stalin, Joseph, 116, 120
Stalingrad, 110
Stanley, Henry, 57–58
Stanton, Edwin, 49, 50
Stars and Stripes, The, 87, 115
Steamfitters Union, 130
Steinbeck, John, 120
Stickney, Joseph L., 69
Stockholm "War Crimes Trial," 126–27
Stowe, Leland, 104
Stret, Joseph M., 20
Sweden, 126–27
Swope, Herbert Bayard, 118

Tampa, Fla., 70
Tarkington, Booth, 78
Thomas, Isaiah, 1–3
Thompson, John H., 111
Thyen, George, 128
Timoshenko, Semyon, 116
Towne, Benjamin, 16
Tremain, Frank, 106–7
Tremain, Mrs. Frank, 107
Trenton, battle of, 14
Twain, Mark, 20–21, 60–61
Tweed, William Marcy, 55–56

United Press (UP), 90. *See also* specific correspondents

Van Buren, Martin, 26
Vermillion, Bob, 121
Verne, Jules, 62, 63
Vicksburg, Miss., 41
Vicksburg *Sentinel,* 20

Vietnam, 126, 130
Villa, Pancho, 84
Villard, Oswald Garrison, 40–41
Virginia City, Nev., *Territorial Enterprise,* 59–60
Virginia *Gazette,* 4

Wainwright, Jonathan, 108
Wales, Hank, 88–89
Walker, Walton H., 121–22
Walney, USS, 110
Walsh, Denny, 130
Wardman, Irvin, 66
Washington, George, 14–15, 16–17
Washington *Daily News,* 129
Washington *Globe,* 25–26
Washington *National Intelligencer,* 19–20, 27
Wasp, USS, 109
Watkins, Kathleen Blake, 72
Wehrwein, Austin C., 128
Whiskey Ring, 56
Whittier, John Greenleaf, 36
Wilhelmshaven, 111
Wilkeson, Samuel, 39, 45–46
Williams, Wythe, 82, 87–88
Wilson, Henry B., 90, 91
Wilson, Woodrow, 94
Winchell, Walter, 101–3
Wing, Henry A., 47–53
Woollcott, Alexander, 87
World War I, 79–91
World War II, 104–5, 106–17

Yank, 115
"Yellow Kid, The," 65–66
Young, Brigham, 33

Zenger, John Peter, 10–12

Thomas Fleming, author of BEHIND THE HEADLINES: GREAT MOMENTS IN AMERICAN NEWSPAPER HISTORY, is also the author of *All Good Men, A Cry of Whiteness, The Man from Monticello* and *Now We Are Enemies,* a Literary Guild Selection. Born in Jersey City, educated in parochial schools there and graduated from Fordham University, he began his writing career as a reporter on the *Yonkers Herald Statesman* in 1951. In 1954 he joined the staff of *Cosmopolitan* magazine and four years later attained the position of Executive Editor, which he held until 1960, when he became a full-time writer. Mr. Fleming, recipient of the 1963 Brotherhood Award of the National Conference of Christians and Jews for magazine writing, is married to the former Alice Mulcahey of Yonkers, herself a writer of children's books. The Flemings have four children and live in New York City.